# PRAISE

"I love that Jason is honest about business! It takes determination and patience. Jason's coaching style is down-to-earth and easy to understand to lay people. Those that are new to business will be able to implement the scenarios discussed with ease! I sent him an email not quite understanding a few things and Jason took it upon himself to call me. After our call I was able to relax and understand the process better. I really appreciate Jason for reaching out to me the way he did. I'm lucky to have such an awesome coach!!! I felt confident that I could effectively apply the strategies my coach taught me. Jason Miller is wonderful!"

7-Figure Coaching Student

"Jason Miller has been a pleasure to work with. Once I found out we had military background we hit it off. Jason has been great explaining everything from the beginning. We have worked together to where I have my autoresponder set up completely and I'm ready to start building my email list for my business. He has been great with checking over my work to make sure I'm doing it right and when I'm not he explains in detail of what I need to change and why. Awesome Coach!! What is great is I can always send a text through Skype, and he always gets back to me quickly. It's nice to know he is just a click away.

What I like about Jason is I feel we will be friends even after our coaching lessons are over with. He is just that type of a person that makes you feel like a friend. He doesn't overpower you with information and makes sure you're comfortable with what you need to be doing. He makes you feel comfortable to talk to and ask those dumb questions. All I can say is I am thankful to have Jason Miller as my coach. Perfect fit!"

7 - Figure Coaching Student

"Jason gets right to business AND is a great listener AND effectively moves the iceberg (me) in the right direction. It's great to know that I'm getting MAXIMUM value from every minute during my coaching sessions. Also, Jason's "no hype" approach to coaching is refreshing and effective. His ability to communicate with laser focus helps expand my vision AND confidence about my Internet business. This comes in handy when I'm spinning my wheels from information overload. Jason's mastery of skills necessary to be a coach are GREATLY APPRICIATED! Looking forward to all future sessions!"

7-Figure Coaching Student

"I have had 2 sessions with Jason Miller, plus I've gone through his training on YouTube. He is EXCELLENT. Jason is very easy to understand and very encouraging during our sessions. I was very impressed with Jason's dedication to his trainees as he was even doing coaching sessions with them on Skype while on vacation. Now that is DEDICATION!!"

His willingness to talk to us on our level and coach us through our questions and problems is amazing. We are looking forward to continuing our training with him when we arrive home from our trip. Jason doesn't hold anything back when he is teaching us, and we really appreciate his openness. He is an Amazing Asset to have on your side in business and definitely to me."

7 - Figure Coaching Student

"Jason may have been the absolutely perfect coach selection for me. I like his instruction methods and his ability to reduce the complex to the understandable.

"His willingness to happily spend more than the allocated time is much appreciated by me.

"Friendly, punctual, knowledgeable, disciplined in staying on topic till I fully understood the subject. Always willing to critique and advise on copy. Provided answers to questions outside of the allotted and required time allocation. All in all a true professional who tells it like it is.

"With still many more sessions available to me with Jason I would have to say I am deeply impressed with the caliber and integrity of his coaching. I'm happy that Jason is my coach. I believe it's a good fit."

7 - Figure Coaching Student

"I love Jason. He is clear and well spoken. He understands my level and talks to where I am at in my business. He is patient with me and answers all my questions. He works well with my learning pace and me. He often spends more than the allotted with me on the Skype. He is thorough and keeps us on the subject matter. He is understanding of where I am at and able to move at my pace. Very open and willing to help me improve. Jason is a strong individual with good skills and good with people. I am very pleased with him and glad he is my coach."

7 - Figure Coaching Student

# Combat Boots to Marketing Pro

## The Secret Methods to Creating Wealth Online, and How You Can Become a Successful Entrepreneur

Jason T. Miller

ISBN: 978-1-64184-842-8 (paperback)
ISBN: 978-1-64184-843-5 (hardback)
ISBN: 978-1-64184-844-2 (ebook)

## *Dedication*

This book is dedicated to all aspiring entrepreneurs that are, "Stepping Outside The Box" within their own lives and was designed to help those that are willing to step outside their comfort zone and become the CEO of their own lives.

I would further like to dedicate this book to the military members and family members (my brothers and sisters) that have paid the ultimate sacrifice. The world is forever in your debt.

I wrote this book to bring forward new possibilities in your life as an entrepreneur. I want to give you the encouragement, tips, tricks, and strategies I have used as an entrepreneur. I encourage you to think big and allow your creative imagination to skyrocket you to new heights in your life.

*"Risk more than others think is safe. Dream more than others think is practical."*

–Howard Schultz, Starbucks CEO

# CONTENTS

# FAMOUS QUOTES ABOUT ENTREPRENEURSHIP

*"My biggest motivation? Just to keep challenging myself. I see life almost like one long university education that I never had; everyday I'm learning something new."*

–Richard Branson

*"Twenty years from now you will be more disappointed by the things that you didn't do than by the ones you did do. So throw off the bowlines. Sail away from the safe harbor. Catch the trade winds in your sails. Explore. Dream. Discover."*

–Mark Twain

*"Entrepreneurship is living a few years of your life like most people won't so you can spend the rest of your life like most people can't."*

–Warren G. Tracy's student

# ACKNOWLEDGMENTS

I would like to personally thank my mentors that have helped me make this book possible and have influenced my decision-making process as an entrepreneur. I appreciate each of you and you know exactly who you are. Thank you for the valuable time, input, and feedback that you have provided me as a business owner and entrepreneur.

Without your guidance, counsel and occasional tough love, our business would not be where it is today.

A very special thank you goes to Tom Still for writing the foreword to this book. Thank you for your mentorship through the process of writing this book.

My family is forever in your debt, and we appreciate you very much!

# SPECIAL SHOUT OUTS

To my wife, Erika. I wouldn't be where I am without you. You are a very special woman, and I love you!

To my four wonderful children: Briana, Haylee, Barrett, and Vivian. I love all of you!

To my ultimate mentor and great friend T.J. Rohleder. You have been an inspiration and the best mentor one could ever ask for. Thank you for all of your mentorship and guidance.

To my family. All of you have influenced my life in one way or another, especially my father, Terry. Thank you for raising me tough and resilient and being there for me.

To every soldier that I have ever served with. "Those of you I respect, you know who you are! I salute you. Thank you for your service.

# FOREWORD

*Are energy and knowledge the tools for your success?*

The answer to this question can only be found within oneself. To believe in a principal or the drive to strive for a better life can often be found closer than you think. So this is where the story begins. I had the pleasure of working with Jason T. Miller during his military career, although being a veteran of over 20 years myself, I often come across individuals that have ideas and methodologies that sometimes work and sometimes not. As time went on and I worked with Jason on various government projects, I observed a fire within this individual and a drive to succeed in the things that he started. As we worked on these projects, various things would happen that required modifications or changes before completion to improve on the product that we were creating.

During our time working together I observed and happened to notice that Jason would always discuss various ideas about his private ventures. So I sat back and listened to his marketing plans and service thoughts. At that time, my thoughts were to kickback and observe Jason's business strategies. As time went on Jason and I continue to discuss his business strategy. We discussed his various product lines and reselling marketing ideas. I know that there were many times after working with Jason, I would go home and discuss with my wife a unique individual and his drive and energy that he would put forth in his work.

It was not too long after that when Jason introduced me to his wife Erika which is also a co-business owner with Jason. As time moved on, I noticed that Jason and Erika were well-suited for one another and wanted the same things out of life. Also, this is when I started to notice their success in business service marketing strategy. Although everything was looking positive, I still had my doubts and misunderstanding of what they were trying to achieve.

## Energy

Continuing to observe Jason and Erika in their business opportunity in marketing, I started to realize that maybe I had become tired and lacking in my creative thinking ability. Although I have owned a number of businesses and always considered myself a creative thinker, I was still lacking the fundamental energy to strive for a greater opportunity in market strategy. Jason and I would discuss quite frequently on a weekly basis a multitude of different ideas. I started to realize at that point Jason and Erika were becoming very successful in this new life and career that they had chosen.

As we continue to discuss various business thoughts. I realized that my creative thought process was starting to come back and improve. It was as if, the cobwebs and the rusty gears in my brain were starting to regenerate. Now I know this may seem a bit crazy but it's true.

As I discussed with my wife, the concepts and strategies that Jason and myself had were really energizing me to pick up the pace. This is why although you may have the energy inside of you, you might not know how to tap into that source. This is where I believe Jason and Erika and their business marketing strategy can assist you in finding the energy and restore your creative thoughts and abilities to move forward in your business opportunity.

## Knowledge

One should ask themselves, Do I have the knowledge I need to become successful? Well at least I thought I did, until I started observing Jason and Erika's business marketing strategy. I know you're probably saying right now "marketing" is not that hard. Well maybe you're right, but is it bringing you the financial success that you desire? One must ask, is there no room for improvement? If your answer is yes, you could use some improvements. I believe you should tap into Jason and Erika Miller marketing methods and strategies. The thing with knowledge is:

1. No knowledge is unacceptable
2. Some knowledge is better than no knowledge
3. More knowledge is better than some knowledge

Your business success depends on the knowledge that you present to your clients. This is where Jason and Erika assist in helping others achieve their success.

I would like to leave you with this thought. Do you have the energy and the knowledge to move forward with your business ventures? I know I did, and this is why Jason and Erika have been a big success for me. Teaming with them has expanded me in being a better entrepreneur in marketing services. Kicking me back into my creative thinking ability and providing a vast array of business marketing strategies.

Respectfully,

Tom Still
STILLusa, LLC

# CHAPTER 1

## MY STORY AND HOW I GOT STARTED IN BUSINESS

My name is Jason Miller, and I grew up in a small town on the border of Montana and North Dakota. I grew up on a farm as a hard-working kid raising crops and tending livestock with my family.

We were a small farm operation that just made enough to live a comfortable life. My parents worked very hard to provide for my sister and I, but it was certainly a tough road and a lot of hard work for them. We were not poor by any means, but we fell in a common category like many, we lived comfortably.

There were certainly no luxury cars and fancy houses and certainly no beachfront property for a summer vacation home. But this taught me a valuable life lesson growing up…. Appreciate the things you do have.

My family has a long bloodline of military service and has served in many of the wars we have fought. Following a time-honored tradition, I joined the military at the ripe age of 17 and shipped off for basic training upon graduation from high school.

JASON T. MILLER

Upon completion of all my training as a new Infantryman I was assigned to my first duty station. I spent the first part of my career in a light Infantry Recon Platoon as a Scout Sniper and Spotter.

I have made many moves over the course of my 20+ year career in the military. I have seen many things and have been to many places both good and bad just like many of my fellow brothers and sisters at arms. Then my life changed. I met my beautiful wife Erika who was also in the military.

We instantly related being in the military and because of our common goals and desires for a future of personal, professional, and financial independence. We moved from place to place as we all do in the military and realized that there has to be more.

After my wife got out of the military she found it very difficult to start a career. She would just begin to climb the ladder of success just in time for us to make that next move to another duty station. So she did what many military spouses do and went to college. She now has two master's Degrees but has never fully been able to utilize her education because of moving every few years.

Like many, she has worked in jobs not careers. My wife and I have always had that sense that there was something better out there waiting for us. We have discussed many times the possibilities of starting our own business full-time and giving up the hectic life of the military. At the time I was well over the 10-year journey of my military career, so it made sense to stick it out and get my 20-year retirement.

So fast-forward to 2014. I deployed to Afghanistan and spent some time there assisting the Afghan Army rebuild and take control of their country. It was there that I had an absolute epiphany as I was sitting on my makeshift bed inside a

2

sweatbox plywood room that was about the size of a prison cell. This is where the initial seeds were planted in my mind to take action and start our own online business. I knew I was quickly approaching retirement and needed to figure out a plan for our next chapter in life.

So there I was on the crappy makeshift bed with crappy internet service searching for opportunities to make money with an online business. I did the research but ultimately set it aside as an idea upon redeployment home.

When I returned home and settled back into normal life, Erika and I began to reengage the discussion of starting our sustainable online business. I remembered the research I did on many business models when I was deployed, so we did more research and decided to give it a shot.

This was an opportunity for me to do when I retired and also an opportunity for my wife to have a meaningful career working from home. We decided to become an unstoppable team and start our own online business.

We wanted to create a lasting income that would allow us to spend more time together as a family and not have to live the normal 9-5 lifestyle dealing with traffic day-in and day-out and having to report to a "boss." We wanted to become the CEOs of our own lives by taking our years of military experience and pouring it into a solid business model.

Our goal has always been to earn a full-time income online and be the CEOs of our own lives. So we jumped in feet first and 100 miles an hour. We started attending business training, which was very relatable since training is second nature for us "military types." The training and business summits that we attended were easy to get through because it walked us through the initial process of setting up our online business step by step.

We reached out to industry leaders for mentorship to help walk us through the things we didn't fully understand.

The one thing that set us apart was our consistent drive to succeed at anything we do. The military has deeply instilled this attribute in both of us. This has served us well in our business ventures and has helped us reach new heights in our lives.

My wife and I will never have to work "normal" employee jobs ever again. Our military careers have been a driving factor in our success because of that sheer will to succeed. Like many, I enjoyed the last 20+ years of my military career. It has been exciting, rewarding and has taken care of my family in many ways that the outside world cannot relate to.

However, we have now found a new start and a new journey down another path in our lives as successful entrepreneurs helping others find their success in life.

Now, to be honest business up to this point was not completely new. In 2001 I started my first eBay business online. I nurtured this business for almost 14 years, and it was also very successful. Running a multiple six figure eBay business is not an easy task. Imagine shipping thousands of items from your home without a central storage and shipping facility!

eBay was a fun and exciting business, but it grew out of control. I often tell people we got too big for our britches in the physical products niche. Then we found the power of digital products and the ability to license products as affiliate marketers.

This really changed the game and is how we have been able to build a sustainable online business today. Coupled with our own digital learning products of our own, we can license other company's products and sell them for a cut of the final cost of the sale.

Now that we are established in the industry, we have been able to create multiple six figure quarterly sales in our business through cultivating multiple income streams. In this book I will show you some of my best tips and tricks to help you do the very same thing! Read every page of this book and feel free to reach out to us on our website anytime!

# Chapter 2
## My Experience Coupled With Masterminds

Experience? Is experience really necessary to start a business? Well, I would say to a degree that the answer is yes. Do you really need a master's degree in business? Absolutely not! When I started my first business back in the late 90's and early 2000's I had -0- business experience. I later went on to get my degree in business management which I can tell you has contributed a big goose egg to the success of my companies.

Experience is best had through two things:

- Trial and error by self-teaching

- Attending summits, seminars, and masterminds

The best experience you will ever get in business will be to get in there, get dirty and experience failure alongside success. You will experience both and it does not matter what business you are in. The one thing business is not is butterflies and pixie dust. Many business owners will not share their very rough times. The fact is that all businesses go through ups and downs and left and rights! Self-study will be so important to your success. Study other successful people and model what they are doing. Often time's people try to recreate the wheel. This normally ends up in a massive failure. A small percentage of people who do start-ups with their own ideas actually succeed!

This is why you need to take a hard long look at what your options are and how you can exploit a business opportunity that makes sense for you. Formal education is great but doing thing through exploration are lifelong learning events. I have spent many years self-learning. In our online business one of the best learning tools out there is YouTube. I always tell people that I have my second degree from YouTube! This is a great way to learn and consume information in a very quick way.

Second is the power of Masterminds. These business building summits are great for many reasons. They are a great place to learn business strategies from 7 and 8 figure business owners that have "Figured it out" for lack of better terms. It also gives you the opportunity to meet people like you and share business ideas and help each other.

I actually met my very first mentor at a Mastermind and he helped me take my business from a hundred dollars a day to over one thousand dollars a day in a very short period of time. The power of a mentor and or coach is massive.

Lastly, attending these Masterminds can help position you within the Niche you are working in. You may be able to offer your services to some of the people attending. You may even be able to do Joint Venture deals with some of the other attendees of the Mastermind or summit.

So, do not count out this avenue for your new or existing business. Now, attendance to these summits or masterminds can be extremely expensive. With airfare and tickets to the event you can easily exceed

$10K for tickets. Sounds scary but it's all a tax deduction so don't let this stop you from attending an event that could possibly take your business to an entirely different level.

# CHAPTER 3

## GETTING YOUR OWN BUSINESS STARTED "WARM UP"

This chapter is all about getting started. Deciding what niche you plan to break into is the first step and you will want to research this heavily before starting any opportunity. Once you have a nice list of niche ideas, section two will help you analyze the list of niches and "prune" it down to only the most profitable niches.

We hope this information will aid you in your Internet marketing journeys. You may want to use it as a resource guide whenever you're looking to expand your business, so keep it on your desk or somewhere it'll be easy to find. At the end of this book we will provide you with many resources that you can use when setting up your business. It's taken years and lots of experience to learn these methods and resources that are compiled in this book.

Niche ideas are all around you, offline and online. I'm about to share with you 21 resources and ways to get good ideas for niches. Get out a pad and a pen and make a list of potential niches because you're about to discover literally thousands of them. I want you to write down the ones you resonate with. Sure there are profitable niches everywhere, but the niche you choose should be something you're at least interested in or already know about.

You don't need to be an absolute expert in a niche to break into it. However, it helps to have interest in it since you'll be doing business in that niche every day. If a niche bores you to death, then not only will it be hard to get motivated to do any work, but your lack of passion will show to potential customers and website visitors. Another thing to consider is to choose only a niche that you feel comfortable with. For example, Gambling niches are very profitable, but you may or may not feel comfortable with it.

The same goes for any other niche you may not be comfortable with such as Pay Day Loans. It's lucrative, but if you can't sleep well at night promoting Pay Day loan offers, then don't touch that niche even with a 50-foot pole.

For hobby niche ideas, check out Magazines.com and browse the various categories. If there's enough interest in a subject that there's a popular magazine based around it, then you may have a profitable niche on your hands! Also, if you happen to have a subscription to any of the magazines at magazines. com, then you can find great niche ideas by checking out the paid ads inside the magazines.

You can search CPA (Cost Per Action) offers that will give you plenty of niche ideas at Offer Vault. One of the best parts about Offer Vault is that you don't even have to search for anything to get profitable niche ideas. Right when you land on the site, you'll see the offers that are paying the highest per lead.

You can get good physical product niche ideas by checking out the Amazon Best Sellers list. You can browse the best-selling products in any category. Another thing you may want to take a look at for niche ideas is the Table of Contents of best-selling books by using the "Look Inside" feature on Amazon.com. There are sub-niches galore to be discovered inside the tables of contents of these books.

The National Enquirer has the most expensive ad space of any print publication, so pay attention to the ads you see inside each issue you read. If advertisers are paying that kind of money to run their ads, then the offers they're running must be hot. Take a look at what they're advertising in these mega expensive advertisements because where there are hot offers, there are hot niche ideas.

You can get some great niche ideas by checking out eBay Pulse, which will tell you the most popular searches and trends on eBay. You can also browse categories and stores on eBay to spark niche ideas. The categories section is one of the most in-depth I've seen, so give it a look and see what niches are out there.

I'm sure you've seen the "For Dummies" books over the years. If a subject has profit potential, then they make a book about it. What most internet marketers don't know is that Dummies. com is an excellent place to get niche ideas by browsing the various "For Dummies" books.

One great way to find out what people are talking about on forums is by using a forum search engine like BoardReader. You can type in a topic like "Weight Loss" and find out what people are talking about in various forum threads. Pay attention to the problems they're talking about and get niches ideas from them, because people pay for solutions to problems.

Flippa is a massive marketplace for buying and selling websites. As you look through the marketplace, pay attention to the expensive sites and ones that are making a profit because if those sites are making a profit, then why can't you have a site in the same niche that makes a profit as well? You can actually reverse engineer these websites in a way, to find out how their links were built, what type of content they have, and who their audience is by using a tool like Quantcast.

If you're a digital products marketer, then you no doubt already know about ClickBank and the ClickBank Marketplace. Besides internet marketing related products, the CB Marketplace is a great place to find niches based on Gravity. Each product in the marketplace has a Gravity Score (Grav), which is a measurement of how many affiliates have had success promoting a product, so you can find some profitable niches by looking at the products with the highest Gravity.

JVZoo is a newer affiliate network but growing by leaps and bounds. I predict it will become one of the major affiliate networks for digital goods across all niches, so you should join and take a look at the products in the marketplace. The best part about JVZoo is you can see the $ Per Click (the Earnings Per Click) of each product, so the higher the EPC, the higher converting it is. Products with the highest EPCs may give you good ideas for niches that have high converting products.

You can find niche ideas by also browsing the Pay Dot Com marketplace. Pay Dot Com is another digital products affiliate network like ClickBank and JVZoo, bigger than JVZoo yet smaller than ClickBank. The best niche ideas you can get from Pay Dot Com will come from the Top Sellers section.

You may or may not be a fan of infomercials, but nonetheless, they are great for conjuring up niche ideas! When you see an infomercial running multiple times, then chances are that infomercial is profitable. Try to figure out who the ideal customer is for that product. You can actually promote many of these products you see in infomercials in CPA networks like Wolf Storm Media.

You'll get a good idea of what topics are hot at any given moment by using Google Trends. It's also a good idea to type in subjects such as "weight loss" into Google Trends, because you'll find related news articles. You can get some great niche ideas from those news articles. Just beware that trends come and go, obviously, so you may not want to base an entire business on trends.

When you're looking to find out what kind of problems people are having and what solutions they're looking for, Yahoo! Answers can be an almost magical tool.

If you have no idea what you're looking for, then you can browse categories to find potential niche ideas.

If you have a question in mind, then type it into the search box to see what related questions people are asking and try to find the most pressing problems.

Shopping.com is where consumers go to compare products. You'll get niche ideas by exploring their list of Most Popular Products and Popular Pages. Here's one I found that I never would've thought of on my own: Wedding Corsages.

Yahoo! Shopping can give you great ideas for profitable niches with their Shopping Insider articles. Looking at the front page right now I'm getting ideas like Prom Styles and Valentine's Day Gifts. Browse articles by category and you'll end up with a good list of possible niches.

Although Ezinearticles.com got drilled by Google's Panda update, it is still a massive resource for niche ideas for you to take a look at. You'll get niche ideas by browsing different categories and seeing what these authors are writing about. If a particular author has many posts, pay attention to what subjects he or she is writing about because nobody writes that many articles for no reason. There may be profit potential.

The Google Keyword tool can be used to find sub-niches galore. (Do a Google search for "Google Keyword Tool"). When you have a keyword like "weight loss," type it into the Google Keyword tool, then select "only show ideas closely related to my search terms."

You'll start to see long-tail keywords related to the keyword that will begin to dig deeper and find sub-niches.

AdSense Sandbox is a fun site that will show you AdSense ads that are running on sites related to the subject you submit. When you see the ads that are running and what products and services are being promoted, you should start getting good niche ideas.

Pay close attention to the similarities of products, you may be onto something if you see the same type of product over and over again.

If you're looking for niche ideas related to Health in particular, then Bottom Line Publications is an excellent resource. When you go to the site, browse the subjects of their books and newsletters because they are big-time direct marketers. If these niches are responsive to their direct marketing tactics, then they may be responsive to yours as well.

Mixrank will show you PPC ads that are running in various niches when you submit an advertiser, keyword, or publisher into the field. The best part is Mixrank will tell you how long an ad has been running. The longer an ad has been running, generally the more profitable that offer is, so you can see how you can get some niche ideas that are more likely to be profitable. There's a free and a paid version, but the paid version is unnecessary with what we're trying to accomplish here.

## Part 2: Pruning your list of niches

By now you should have a monster list of potentially profitable niches if you went through each resource. No worries if your list is small from only using a couple of the resources. Now we're going to take your list and "prune it." We'll prune it down to the niches of your liking by analyzing them. We're not going to analyze them by using exact data or an exact science.

No niche is perfect, but there are many things to consider when deciding to do internet marketing in a niche. The most important part of this process is finding out the things that appeal most to YOU when it comes to each niche. Use the following 21 Questions when determining whether a niche is for you or not. Some of the questions are about the profit potential of a niche. Other questions are about how easy it's going to be for you to reach your target audience on a daily basis.

Then there are questions about how fast you can grow and become a force in any given niche market. If a niche doesn't sit with you after asking these 21 questions, then delete it from your list. By the end you will have a handful of niches left to choose from.

Keep in mind that there are more questions than just these 21 questions you can consider when selecting a niche. These happen to be the questions that are important to us based on our experience with internet marketing. Besides having a general interest in a niche and being comfortable with it ethically, I want a niche to have profit potential, potential to generate easy traffic, and potential for fast growth.

## Question #1: Are there multiple products in the niche?

The first question you want to ask yourself is, are there a lot of good products? You want to know this because you may quickly run out of good products to offer to your website visitors or e-mail list subscribers. If you're running AdSense or selling ad space on your website or selling ad space in your e-mail newsletter, then that's one thing. But if you're going to be depending on making commissions, then it's vital to have multiple offers you can promote.

## Question #2: How big is the problem your prospect is having?

If it's not a hobby niche, how big is the problem the prospects are having? Is the problem they're having big enough that they'd be willing to part with their hard-earned money to get a solution? Maybe someone would be willing to pay for pain relief, but they wouldn't be willing to pay to solve a lesser problem.

## Question #3: Are there potential JV partners in the niche for explosive growth?

Here's something not many marketers consider when selecting a niche. Are there potential Joint Venture partners already in the niche? Are all of them so big that they would never consider doing a JV deal with you? Or are they so small that it wouldn't matter if they did a JV deal with you? There's no faster way to grow a business than by using Joint Venture deals, so it's something to consider.

## Question #4: Does it make sense to build a list in the niche or not?

Are other internet marketers in the niche building an e-mail subscriber list? Would it make sense to build a list in the niche? You may or may not want to get into a niche where it's a must to build a list in order to make nice profits. Take a look around at the competitors and see if they have opt-in forms on their websites or not. Join their lists and see what it would be like to market in that niche.

## Question #5: How expensive is available ad inventory in the niche?

One major thing you have to consider before getting into a new niche is how easy it will be to reach your target audience. If you're looking to pay for traffic, then you'll want to see how expensive the ad inventory is for that market. For example, you'll find the costs vary when bidding on keywords and URLs using CPV networks like LeadImpact and also when bidding on PPC keywords with Google AdWords.

## Question #6: Will it be easy to generate free traffic in this niche?

If you're looking at going the free traffic route, then take a look around at how easy (or hard) it would be to reach your target prospects in a particular niche using free methods.

You can use the Google Keyword Tool to discover generally how competitive keywords are in a niche. Also try to do some digging around and find out if your competitors are successfully using other free sources like YouTube, Twitter, and Facebook. If they can do it, then why not you?

## Question #7: Are there high-end products or services at $1,000 or more in the niche?

Are there products or services being sold at $1,000, $5,000, or even $10,000 in a niche?

Not many niches have customers who actively spend $1,000 or more on a single product or service. If you can find many offers in your niche in those price ranges, then that's a good sign that you can make easy money in your niche. Because in a niche where high end products are being sold often, you'll find it's easier to make 1 sale at $1,000 than 100 sales at $10.

## Question #8: Are there continuity programs like membership sites in the niche?

It's easier to make dependable income when there are continuity programs in a niche. I'm talking about membership sites, subscriptions, etc. They are especially lucrative when there are services that customers need and will keep paying for month after month.

Webhosting and auto-responder services come to mind.

## Question #9: How fast do vendors pay out in the niche and do they pay out at all?

When vendors don't pay out fast or if they don't pay at all, then that can cripple your business in itself. That's why I recommend staying away from any affiliate programs that aren't on networks like ClickBank, for the most part. There are exceptions to the rule.

Many product vendors wait up to 90 days to pay out commissions, and many don't pay out at all because either they're dirty or they're not responsible enough with their money.

If the only available affiliate programs in your niche aren't on affiliate networks, then my advice is to avoid them like the plague. There are exceptions to this just choose carefully.

## Question #10: Are exact match domains available in the niche?

While this isn't a must, it can give you an edge when it comes to free traffic from Google.

An exact match domain is a domain name (.com preferably) that matches a keyword you want to rank for in Google. One easy way to find whether there are exact match domains available in your niche is to take your keyword list and copy and paste it into GoDaddy Bulk Domain Register. You can use that feature on GoDaddy to find out whether there are exact match domains available without actually buying the domains through GoDaddy.

## Question #11: Could you create a product in this niche?

Having your own product gives you maximum leverage in a niche. You can create cross promotion deals with JV partners and you can sit back and let your affiliate army crush your offer with traffic all day long. If it's a physical product you must create in a niche, then that may be something you can't do. As for digital products, if you don't have the expertise in a niche, then there may be Private Label Rights material available on the web that you can use to aid you in creating a respectable product.

## Question #12: Will it be easy to build your authority in the niche?

Having your own product is honestly the ultimate way to build authority in a niche.

Another way is by having JV partners who has customers associate you with, so you're borrowing your JV partner's credibility in a way. A popular blog can also give you authority in a niche. Are there already authority blogs in the niche you're looking at? If so, then you may also be able to have one yourself.

## Question #13: Do you already have knowledge of this niche?

It's much easier to enter a niche when you already have knowledge or expertise in it.

You don't have to be an expert, but being an intermediate is enough to share what you know information-wise. If you have a burning desire to learn more about a niche, then that can help in entering a niche as well. In that role you're more of a reporter than an authority figure.

## Question #14: Are people spending money in this niche?

Many hobbies are popular and solutions for problems are searched for all over the net, but that doesn't mean they spend money on it. In this case you'll need to verify whether there are buyers in the niche or not by checking out bestseller lists using the resources we talked about earlier. We will include a resource page at the end of this book. It's easy to make the mistake of choosing a popular yet unprofitable niche, so make sure you "do your homework" on this.

## Question #15: Is coaching being sold in the niche?

Everyone knows there's good money to be made in coaching, whether internet marketing coaching, life coaching, etc. Coaching packages are sold for thousands of dollars, so if you're a good lead generator then you can either sell your own coaching packages or generate leads for coaches who do sell packages. They can afford to spend more on leads you generate for them because they're charging high prices.

## Question #16: Are there pay per lead offers in this niche?

Promoting Pay Per Lead Offers can be much more profitable than Pay Per Sale Offers, which you may be accustomed to. It's easier to get someone to fill out a form than buy something. If there are Pay Per Lead Offers in the niche, then you may have an easier time converting your traffic into money.

## Question #17: Will it be easy to stand out from the crowd in this niche?

Some niches have a crazy amount of competition, but that doesn't mean you should be scared to enter them. Is there a way you can stand out from the crowd in a competitive niche? Think about it, because standing out can help you stomp your competition into the ground. This has a lot to do with positioning. Maybe you have expertise in a sub-niche that you can share that will put you head and shoulders above your competition.

## Question #18: Are there webinars or teleseminars in the niche?

Webinars and teleseminars generate sales like crazy, but not every niche is responsive to them. In any niche you need a vehicle to make money, so if there are webinars and teleseminars in a niche, then chances are you can do the same thing or promote them as an affiliate. While the average conversion rate of a sales letter online is roughly 1%, webinars and teleseminars convert generally around 10% or more.

## Question #19: Are there call centers in this niche?

What converts even higher than webinars and teleseminars, is one- on-one phone selling, so keep an eye out for it in the niche you're assessing. Just beware that many call centers are dirty. However, just using the phone to sell will increase your conversion rates to as much as 50% depending on how the lead was generated. If there are call centers in a niche, then you can also use the power of the telephone to close more sales.

## Question #20: Is this niche related to Health, Wealth, or Relationships?

If the niche you're looking at is related to Health, Wealth, or Relationships, then you may have a mass market on your hands. Health, Wealth, and Relationships-related products and services are known to be cash cows. Also, the traffic potential is generally higher when related to Health, Wealth, and Relationships.

### Question #21: Are there many searches in Google in this niche?

Take a look at the Google Keyword Tool (type "Google Keyword Tool" into Google to find it). If you see low traffic levels for keywords in your niche, then it doesn't make much sense to choose this niche. Sure the competition is likely low. However, there's usually a reason for that. There is a lack of customers.

## Part 3: Broad brush of traffic

Now, let's just do a broad brush on traffic. There are some nice new advertising sources in this book for you to discover and some of them are huge. Others are smaller yet legit.

I'm talking about Solo Ads, PPC, PPV, as well as some untraditional types of advertising like paying for blog posts. I hope you'll find many new ad networks and places to buy ads from that you didn't previously know about.

It's important to note that you're not going to need all of these sources. You could spend millions of dollars with just one or a handful of these select sources. Think of these traffic sources we discuss as a mini guide to the available ad inventory out there that you may have not known about. Crack it open whenever you're looking to buy some traffic.

Before we get started with these ad sources, I also wanted to tell you that you can get a world-class education in buying traffic for free.

One way is to join a CPA network such as Wolf Storm Media and take their free trainings. Another way is to learn all you can from the actual ad network sites that you'll discover here.

It's also vital to get some ads running and track everything using a program such as ClickMagick. You honestly don't need a $2,000 course to learn about internet advertising because the best way to learn is to get out there and do it.

While you can learn the basics from someone else, the real learning comes from your experience. When you're tweaking ads, when you're tweaking your bids, when you're crunching your numbers and looking at your metrics and adjusting... That's when you're REALLY learning! So take everything you learn from others like a grain of salt.

Take these advertising sources, go out there, and generate all the traffic your little heart desires.

## JV Rocket and "Tier 1 Solo Ads"

With JV Rocket you can buy a solo ad that will go out to a double opt-in list of 226,000 subscribers for the price of $2,500. Your ad goes out to customers who have purchased ClickBank products in the Make Money niche such as Get Google Ads Free, Health Biz in a Box, Forced Money, and Top Secret Magic Code. You'll also reach affiliates for ClickBank products such as Get Google Ads Free, Health Biz in a Box, Forced Money, Top Secret Magic Code, Cash Making Power Sites, Top Secret Fat Loss Secret, and Top Secret Car Secret.

Many of the top Internet Marketing and Make Money niche gurus are using JV Rocket to build their lists and also to directly mail to their hot offers. $2,500 is a nice chunk of money to risk, so before testing a JV Rocket you'll want to make sure you have tested sales material. You'll also want to be sure that your offer would be a good match for the type of customers who would buy the type of products I just mentioned above.

This doesn't mean that your offers must be similar, but it does mean that the same demographic would order your product. The downside of this solo ad source is that there are no guaranteed number of visitors you'll get. The upside is that if you have an offer that's on fire and would work well with these types of customers then JV Rocket can be a goldmine. Just remember, as with all of these ad sources in this book, you're responsible for your business and the risks you take with buying advertising.

Profiting from paid advertising is simple, but not easy. Here's what I mean. It would be easy to blow through $10,000 on JV Rockets. The inventory is there waiting for you to order anytime you want. However, it would be wise to test your sales funnel out buying solo ads on a small scale at $30, $100, or $300 a pop from "Tier 2 Solo Ad" vendors such as the ones on Safe-Swaps.com, SoloAdDirectory.com, or Directory of Ezines.

After you have a tested and proven funnel that works well with the solo ads you've purchased on a small scale, then you may want to consider going big time and ordering what I call "Tier 1 Solo Ads" such as JV Rocket.

JV Rocket isn't the only Tier 1 Solo Advertising available. Here are some more in various niches: Arcamax (General Consumer List), Newsmax, Self Growth, and Nextmark.

LeadImpact and Top CPV Networks Technically TrafficVance is a better quality CPV network than LeadImpact in my opinion, but the barrier to entry with TrafficVance is $1,000.

With LeadImpact, on the other hand, you only need $100 to get started using their massive network. I find it much easier to generate mass targeted traffic with LeadImpact than the other major CPV networks with a low barrier to entry such as Direct CPV and Media Traffic. LeadImpact allows you to buy traffic on a Per View basis. You're essentially buying something similar to popups.

Paying "Per View" means a small window will open on their screen and it will lead to your webpage. Your webpage must fit inside that window. You can bid on keywords or URLs using LeadImpact. When bidding on a keyword, website content will match your keyword and trigger your pop up. When bidding on a URL, visiting that URL will trigger your popup. Depending on your Geo Targeting and the Category/Sub-Category of your offer, the lowest bid you can start with will be as low as .015 to .017.

The downside of LeadImpact is that I don't personally like how they have the minimum bidding set up. For some Sub-Categories you might have a minimum bid of .015 and for others it may be .025.

One cent may not seem like a big difference but when you multiply that 1,000+ times per day, it starts to add up. Small squeeze pages seem to do very well with LeadImpact. They can be your own squeeze pages or a Pay-Per-Lead (PPL) offer in a CPA network.

I find there's not as much inventory in the Make Money and Internet Marketing niches, but there's a ton in large markets that are multiple times bigger.

For example, you can generate a serious amount of traffic on a daily basis to Pay-Per- Lead online gaming offers. Same goes for Weight Loss, Health, and Financial niches.

To find PPL offers to promote, try a CPA offers search engine such as Offer Vault.

With Plenty of Fish ads, you can reach 20,000,000 users on a CPM basis. In case you're not familiar with "CPM," it simply means "Cost per 1,000 impressions of your ad." You'll also be bidding for ad inventory on a CPM basis. The minimum buy is just $25, so you can cheaply give POF Ads a nice test run for as low as $25.

It takes 24 hours or less for your ads to be approved. Image ad sizes include 110x80px, 300x250px, 160x600px and 120x600. Besides the insanely low point of entry at $25 minimum, there's something else about POF Ads that makes your traffic highly targeted.

In-depth demographics targeting is available. You can target prospects based on:

- Country, State/Province, ZIP Code

- Age, Gender

- Education, Profession

- Has Children, Games and Puzzles

- Body Type, Drinking Habits

- Looking to Marry Soon, Ethnicity

- Height, Income, Marital Status

- Religion, Smoking Habits, Hair Color

Your ads are so ultra-targeted that they're not even shown to POF visitors who aren't logged in. Your ad is displayed above the fold as well. With POF Ads you can really go to town with specific dating offers. For instance, imagine targeting

Christians who are looking to date. You can put a Christian Singles offer in front of them.

Do you see how powerful POF Ads can be? Because you have access to so many demographics, your ads don't even have to be about dating. They can be about something totally unrelated but targeted to the demographic you choose.

There are many CPA offers out there related to dating if that's what you want to explore.

Or this is a perfect time for you to start your Dating or Relationships niche empire by generating leads from Plenty Of Fish to your own subscriber list. ClickBank products such as The Magic of Making Up may also do well with POF Ads.

7Search.com is one of my favorites of the "Tier 2 PPC" networks, search engines, and the like. Google, Yahoo, MSN, and Facebook are considered "Tier 1 PPC" in my book. Everything else is Tier 2 PPC the way I see it. The great thing about 7Search is you don't have to worry about Quality Score or other headaches. You set up a landing page, you bid on keywords, and you tweak your campaigns until they're profitable.

If you're looking to generate biz op leads, then you may want to check out Ad Hitz.

With Ad Hitz, you can do site-specific targeting (recommended) on some biz op sites that get serious traffic, such as MyBrowserCash.com that gets 23,1411 unique visitors per day and ClickSense.com that gets 281,360 unique visitors per day.

Now, if you're looking for serious Internet Marketing niche leads, then Ad Hitz may or may not be for you. These leads you generate will be the type that hang out on pay to click sites and probably paid survey sites. This doesn't necessarily mean that these prospects are "low quality" or not serious about business, but it does mean that they're clueless about what you and I know about. So I think it's important to not take advantage of these clueless prospects. Instead, you should show them the light.

For serious Internet Marketing leads who are already more advanced, you'll want to buy an ad at the top of WarriorForum. com or run Warrior Special Offers. There are over 450,000 members on Warrior Forum and growing.

Another option for generating serious Business leads in general is by using LinkedIn Ads. You won't necessarily generate all internet marketing leads there, but there are 130,000,000 business-minded members on LinkedIn to advertise to. 40,000,000 are US based. With LinkedIn Ads you don't have to pay on a PPC basis because they also offer inventory on a CPM basis (cost per 1,000 impressions). It's your choice.

## PayPerPost, Blog Ads, and ReviewMe

You may want to consider blog advertising. This is where your website or your product is promoted on real blogs. PayPerPost is one of them and they connect you with real bloggers out there who are willing to do a write up about your product or site for a fee.

Besides generating the direct traffic from your links, you'll also be building links, except you won't be building links on fly-by-night blog networks that get de-indexed from the search engines in the blink of an eye.

You have complete control over how much you'll spend on a post when you create your listing called an "Opportunity." You also get to select the categories and the Geo Targeting. Blog Ads is another option for advertising on blogs, but it's not contextual like PayPerPost. Here you're buying actual ad space on a time basis. What I mean is you're not buying on a PPC or CPM basis like some of the other sources we've talked about.

You're buying ads based on the amount of time they'll run on the blog.

It's just like buying ad space direct from a webmaster at a fixed rate, only you're doing it through the Blog Ads network. The pricing is set up similar to Text-Link-Ads. Price doesn't go up or down based on the number of impressions or click through on your ad.

ReviewMe is another option with blog advertising, and it can work well to create buzz for your new product or service. You can browse the different blogs at ReviewMe.com and purchase a review of your product or service.

You'll also get the link back to your site, but just keep in mind that these bloggers will do an honest review for you and that review will be permanent. You can also create a listing for what you're looking for if you're looking to be found by bloggers who are looking to review products or services similar to your own.

## AbestWeb, CB, JV Zoo, W+, PDC, DigiResults

If you're advertising to get affiliates, then you'll want to run some ads on AbestWeb, the world's largest affiliate marketing forum. Super affiliates galore hang out on this forum and have their eyes open for hot offers to promote all the time. They can generate traffic all day long, but they don't always have offers that convert, so if your offer is appealing enough to them, then just one super affiliate you get from running an ad can be worth much more than what you paid for the ad. Check out the different advertising options at AbestWeb website. They have all kinds of inventory from banner ads to e-mail blasts to their members.

Getting your digital product listed in the ClickBank Marketplace is also a great way to pick up affiliates who can drive traffic to your site all day and night on a commission basis. With ClickBank, you're technically buying traffic, but it's no risk because you're only paying when someone makes a sale.

Other options have emerged as well including JV Zoo, WSO Pro, PayDotCom, and DigiResults. Honestly, I'm a fan of all those programs just listed. Instead of being paid by ClickBank, you're paid directly upon each sale with PayPal. However, the marketplaces aren't even close to as old or as big as ClickBank. So there are a lot more affiliates waiting in the ClickBank marketplace to see your offer to promote than the others, but you don't get instant PayPal payments.

You can also pick up some affiliates by listing your product in the Warrior Forum Affiliate Programs Database for a small fee. There are more ways to get super affiliates to promote for you. One is by busting your butt putting together a massive product launch and getting listed on sites like JV Notify Pro and Warrior JV. Another way is to simply get the attention of super affiliates by running your offer on networks.

If you throw $10,000 at advertising your offer, then chances are super affiliates are going to see it, and they are always looking for one thing: offers that convert.

## StumbleUpon Ads, PR Web, and Direct CPV

If you know how StumbleUpon works, it's where users click the "Stumble" button, and they are sent from webpage to webpage checking out pages that have been "Stumbled" by other users and are related to their favorite topics. With StumbleUpon Paid Discovery, your webpage becomes part of that Stumbling process. Users land on your landing page while Stumbling through websites and you pay per view. My opinion is it's a bit pricey at this point, but I also think it's a great way for companies to spread brand awareness and it's also potentially good for viral marketing.

Using PR Web is another way to launch a viral marketing or brand awareness campaign.

To tell you the truth, it's also possible to generate a lot of direct traffic as well. Not to mention you can get some serious offline traffic if your press release gets picked up by a newspaper. PR Web allows you to distribute a press release to the far corners of the internet, depending on the package you choose. The important thing to remember when writing the press release is making it newsworthy, so you could technically do a press release for virtually anything that's happening with your website, product, or business.

Whenever you launch a new website, for example, you can create a press release and submit it to PR Web.

You can also do this when you put out a new product. Although Direct CPV was already briefly mentioned in the CPV section, I never pointed out that you can use their Run of Network (normally referred to as RON) traffic for brand awareness and getting viral marketing campaigns off the ground. Run of Network traffic is untargeted, and it runs to all available inventory on the network, so it's an insanely high amount of traffic.

You could blow through thousands of dollars very fast, so be careful with it.

COMBAT BOOTS TO MARKETING PRO

Don't expect to get any good measurable results with Run of Network traffic on Direct CPV. But it is possible to use to get thousands of views on a YouTube video in one day, for instance. Just don't expect to use this type of traffic as you would other types.

## More advertising networks and ad sources

Bravenet Media, MyAds, Her Agency, Indie Click, Batanga, 24/7 Media, BuySellAds, Adfish, Crisp Ads, ExoClick, Adtegrity, Intermarkets, HIRO, Casale Media, Banner Space, Ad On Network, Advertising.com, Yahoo Media Services, AdBuyer.com, Kitara Media, Flux Advertising, Burst Media, Kontera, Clicksor, Pepperjam, TrafficJunky

Opt-Media, Mirago, Miva, Ad Magnet, AdBlade, Tribal Fusion, Pulse360, Marchex, Domain Gateway, AdMarketplace, AdEngage, Chitika, Traffic Taxi, Yes Mail, AdReady, Bidvertizer, Zedo, WeatherBug, Epic Advertising, PCH Games, Popup Traffic, Bardzo Media, ADXDirect, Contextweb, AdBrite

Ok, so these are just some ideas to get your brain muscles working as we continue on.

# Part 4: List building

So moving forward and also another area where we want to get your brain muscle working a bit is list building. A lot of the same things that we were discovering in 2009 still work today, but some don't work as well.

What you're about to get is a combination of new and old list building tactics that I've gathered since 2008 up until now. Just to be clear... I'm going to only share what's working

RIGHT NOW. When I go over the older tactics, I'm going to talk about how well they work RIGHT NOW and how I'm using them TODAY. What I'm going to share with you is not just the tactics themselves, but some I'm going to point out to you and tell you which ones have built me the most subscribers, for example, and which ones are working the best for me right now.

I don't want you to look at this as if it's Just a book of information, I want you to look at it as if it's life changing knowledge because it doesn't matter if it's written on a napkin. It doesn't matter if it's on audio. It doesn't matter if it's on video. It doesn't matter if it's in a PDF. It doesn't matter if someone is teaching it to you one-on-one over the phone or one-on-one through a webinar or through group coaching; it's all information, and this powerful information is the most powerful information that I've discovered through experience.

List building has been the key to our success over the years and we have a lot of people to thank for that, but we mostly have to thank ourselves because we've gone out of our way to explore all of these realms of list building. The first thing you need to know is that business and making sales depends on fresh lead flow. What I mean is you want constant leads coming in. If I were you, I would start aiming to generate something like 250 subscribers per day.

You might be thinking, that's a lot of subscribers, or it's going to be too expensive. Well, there are great paid lead sources; there are also very good free ones that you can use to build up your list to generate 250 or more subscribers per day. Once you hit 250 subscribers per day or more, then it's all a matter of focusing on converting them and then just doing the list building stuff you're doing over and over and over and getting the same results all the time.

Converting them is another thing and I am not going to cover converting leads into sales, it's all about generating lead flow. As I was telling you, I can't stress this enough that the bulk of your money that you make is going to come from the people who are the newest on your list. THE FRESHEST. The older a lead gets, the less responsive they become, generally, especially if you're an affiliate.

Now if you're a product creator and you do classes and such, you may find that some of your older subscribers are the most profitable subscribers you have because they're your own customers who enroll in all of your classes; all of your $1,000 classes and whatnot.

As an affiliate, it's different; you don't have that retention. When you're a product creator, it's easier to keep the retention of your list for some reason.

I've found this to be true and that's one of the reasons why I'm starting to create more and more products now, although over the years I've been mainly just an affiliate. If you are just an affiliate, again, your normal focus should be fresh leads and keeping your leads coming in on a daily basis. That's at least 250 leads a day.

If you're a product creator, you may not need as high of a lead flow, but why not do both? Why not be a creator that keeps retouching the list and also generate 250 subscribers or more to your list? Let's go ahead and get into this because I have tons and tons of list building methods and strategies to cover for you now.

## Public and private JV giveaways

The first one is JV giveaways. JV giveaways haven't changed much as far as public JV giveaways go. You can go to newjvgiveaways.com anytime you want and jump in on any JV giveaways. But what has surfaced since 2011 is something called the private giveaway. There are a lot of little private giveaways taking place that you can be part of all over the internet. You can go to people who are just as big as you are online, and even bigger, and start a private JV giveaway with them.

What I mean is you can get 5 to 10 or more people in on a private giveaway, where no one else can join and be a contributor. This means that the people who are on there, who are contributors, are responsible for generating all the traffic to the giveaway and there is a WordPress plug-in that you can use to host your own private giveaways called WP Venture. So go do a search on Google for WP Venture and it's being sold on the Warrior Forum for chump change, as a Warrior Special Offer.

A giveaway is where a group of contributors come together and submit their gifts. People who come and join the giveaway as members are going to opt into different giveaways and this will add subscribers to your list. If you've been around for a while, you no doubt know what JV giveaways are, and I'm not going to dwell on what JV giveaways are or how they can build good business for you because you can go to a place like newjvgiveaways.com and find out all you need to know about giveaways freely on the net.

But just the fact that I'm pointing you in that direction is pretty valuable because if you're just starting out and you have no money to spend on ads, getting giveaways is a really good way to start, because you can add that first 10, 50, 100 subscribers on your list fairly quickly. Some of these giveaways get up to 30,000 subscribers joining: not to your list, but to the actual giveaway. What happens is the host of the giveaway is going to get the most subscribers.

They're putting the giveaway with all the contributors and setting the dates, and then once the giveaway is live, all the contributors send traffic to the JV giveaway main page, but the host is going to get all the subscribers onto their list. Then the member who just joined will probably see a one-time offer or some kind of offer before they go and see all the different gifts that that contributors have.

So when you're a contributor and you promote one of these JV giveaways through your own link, you often make sales right there before they even get to the gifts. That's one thing about it. My point is if you're just starting out and you don't have much money to buy traffic, then this may be one that you want to master. The truth is, if you became just a master of one of these methods, then you'll generate all the leads you'll ever need.

Let me say that again. If you become the master of just one of these methods I'm going to share with you, then you will generate all the leads you'll ever need. So why not do something like JV giveaways? You can do public ones, you can do private ones, and you can host ones and make the real money. I've hosted a couple and that's where I generated the most leads. You could generate 10,000 leads in one day, 20,000 leads in one day from contributors blasting traffic to your own giveaway.

So just think about that. If you were to jump headfirst into the world of JV giveaways as a contributor to start off with, then one day you may be able to host your own JV giveaways.

## Solo ads

The next list building tactic I want to talk about is solo ads. When I'm actively running solo ads, I'm usually able to generate hundreds of leads per day right now. This may change down the road, but as of right now. Solo ads are cheap, they're effective and very easy because you don't have to worry about landing page quality score or paying per click and keeping an eye on your ads and paying by the click.

What you're getting is an ad that goes out to a subscriber list, so whenever you buy a solo ad; let's say you buy a solo ad for $600 for 1,000 clicks to your site, you pay 60 cents per click to your site and you know exactly how many clicks are going to come to your site and the guy who sends you a solo ad sends an ad out to his email list, which recommends your freebie or your website.

So they're transferring their authority over to you, in a way, that's what makes it the most effective way of generating traffic right now, in my opinion. Because the ads are still cheap, it's very effective for anybody who has the money to risk on it. One place you can find a lot of great solo ad deals is by getting on Skype and talking to different solo ad sellers.

I realize it's not going to be easy just to find a solo ad seller, or any solo ad sellers if you have no clue about the world of solo ads right now, but once you find some solo ad sellers, you want to start connecting with them on Skype and getting into the world of solo ads because you can meet so many different solo ad sellers who will give you great deals on Skype that they don't give outside of Skype. You can find solo ads at one place called udimi.com or soloadsx.com. That's where I would go if I were going to go and look for solo ads right now. The key to have profitable solo ads is your sales funnel.

You want to have the squeeze page that generates the free leads that gives away something. Then you have an upsell from there, which will be a one-time offer for something that's in the $17 to $49 price point, then you want to have upsells from there so you can afford to pay for your solo ads.

Now you may also want to promote things on the download page for your freebies that you're giving away. That way you can come close to breaking even or you can profit directly right away from that solo ad before you even get the subscribers on your list. Although many solo ads I haven't profited from right up front, I made a profit on the backend from promoting strictly to the subscriber list. That's something you have to think about.

A lot of companies in advertising are willing to pay a lot of money upfront and even lose money on the front end because they know they're going to make money on the backend with their follow up marketing, which is what email marketing is all about.

## Ad swaps

So let's move on to ad swaps. Ad swaps are where you send out an ad to your list promoting someone else's squeeze page and then someone else does the same for you to their list. So it's similar to solo ads except for no one is buying anything; you're just trading off ads. The place where everybody has moved to these days is called safe-swaps.com.

There used to be a site called IMadswaps.com, which was like an ad swap forum. There are other forums that kind of emerged in the last few years, and they've pretty much slowed down because of safe- swaps.com. The thing about ad swaps is that it is getting less effective because seeing that it emerged around 2009, that's when everyone was discovering ad swaps and starting to do it. Now people are over-mailing their lists with ad swaps.

They're doing way more ad swaps so they're getting less responses from the subscribers.

Retention rates are going down, click thru rates are going down, but if you still want to generate hundreds of leads per day, you still can do that. The key to profiting from ad swaps is the same key to profiting with solo ads, which is your sales funnel. So if you've got a good sales funnel, you can use it for your ad swaps.

Also, ad swaps are a great way to test your sales funnel before you start buying something like solo ads. You're probably going to get less quality leads from ad swaps than you are solo ads, yet it's still a good indication of whether your sales funnel will convert traffic into sales, and that's what's necessary to profit with ad swaps, because you're not promoting anything that's going to be making money directly to your list; you're promoting someone else's squeeze page, so you're relying on the traffic coming from the JV partner's list to your sales funnel.

Depending on your sales funnel, you can do ad swaps every single day if you want to, become the master of ad swaps, and just tweak your sales funnel and have very good business there. You don't want to overcomplicate marketing. This kind of thinking is really profitable if you could get super focused. Think about how simple this business is right here. You put together a sales funnel. You do ad swaps every day. You test your sales funnel every day until you're converting the maximum number of visitors who land on your page. That in itself is a business no matter what anyone says. So that's what I try to do in my business... SIMPLIFY.

I have a daily routine that I try to simplify down more and more every day until it's just brain-dead stupid, and lately, it has been solo ads because I've found that I'm getting the best returns on solo ads. But if I didn't have any money, I would start off with JV giveaways just to generate 100 subscribers or so, then I would move to safe- swaps.com and I would start ad swapping. That's what I would do if I didn't have any money.

## Click banking

There's also another thing I would want to do if I didn't have any money and I had a small list. This goes out to the small list owners, people who are just starting their lists and what not. If you have a list of 100 people or 1,000 people, you could start doing what's called click banking. It has nothing to do with ClickBank.com but what it is, is you go to a marketer with a huge list, and you say, "I will send you 100 clicks or 1,000 clicks over the course of this month (clicks mean visitors) and what you will do is return those clicks all at once after I'm done."

So what happens is the big marketer with a big list will give you a tracking link to use on all your emails. You'll work hard to build up your traffic to them through that link, and then when you're ready to cash in your clicks you go to them and say, "I'd like to cash in my clicks," and then they send you clicks; they send you as many as you have sent them.

This is very similar to ad swaps, as you can see, but it works out well for small list owners because you can just focus on sending traffic to one big marketer without having to set up all kinds of ad swap deals.

For example, If you have an email follow up series, the first couple of days of your email follow up series could be sending the new people on your list to another marketer who you are click banking with. Now this isn't the greatest advice for product creators.

I don't think that ad swaps or click banking is a great idea for product creators because if you're a product creator, then you can have so much longevity on your own list by just promoting your own products. If you're a product creator, you might want to just focus on paid methods and getting affiliates to promote your stuff, but that's just my opinion and that's what I've seen from experience.

As an affiliate marketer, who doesn't have a ton of products to promote to the list all month, who doesn't crank out many products, it's all about fresh lead flow, like I was saying in the beginning of this chapter. Things like ad swaps and click banking are the mother lode of free, fresh lead flow.

## Free WSOs

Now let's get into another method, which is something I've been doing since 2013 or so, which is running free WSO's. I'm talking about freebies that I give away on the Warrior Forum, which is WarriorForum.com and WSO stands for Warrior Special Offers. So I will give away products on the Warrior Special Offers forum in exchange for opt-ins.

One thing that I've noticed between the Warrior Forum and the leads you may get from ad swaps, click banking, and solo ads is that Warrior Forum traffic is used to buying lower priced products. So your funnel may be a lot different for free WSO's than it will be with ad swaps, click banking, or solo ads. For one of my funnels they get a freebie on the squeeze page, then the OTO after that is a $10 offer, then the OTO after that is another $10 offer.

So you can see I'm keeping it at $10 or less because I know they buy

$10 or less things, whereas with ad swaps, click banking, and solo ads I'll have a freebie, a $9 offer, then to a $97 OTO and then it will go up from there. Good luck trying to sell a $97 to Warrior Forum members because it's not going to happen, unless you have a done-for-you service or something that's worth 25x $97 price points.

It's just a different world there, but the good thing about running free WSO's is that's a business in itself, if you want it to be because you can run free WSO's and then you can promote WSO's as an affiliate to promote programs like offers through WSO Pro, which is at WarriorPlus.com or JVzoo. com or DigiResults.com.

Do you remember how I was talking about making a business just by focusing on one thing? Well this is a business for you too. Think about this. This is all you need to do is to run free WSO's.

You can have six or seven free WSO's for six or seven different freebies that you create, and you can rotate those once a day so that you're launching a new WSO a day, but it's giving away one of your six or seven freebies. You can generate your list like that, and your sales funnel will get you close to breaking even or making a profit right away on the front end, then on the backend you can promote WSO's as an affiliate to your list you've built.

I've been known to have multiple free WSO's that I rotate on a daily basis, and I've done that model before. You see... I get bored with certain things in marketing and then I try different models. I just simplify things and just go at them with a very narrow focus. Right now I might be buying a lot of solo ads and doing what I described in the Solo Ads section, but just months ago, I was buying a lot of free WSO's and trying to get as many leads as I could with that and just promoting WSO's every day and making plenty of money. So once you get that narrow focus and simplify everything, everything becomes clear, and you can make a lot of money just focusing on that.

## PPV/CPV list building

Another way to generate hundreds of leads per day is through something called Pay Per View or Cost Per View advertising. I have a friend who does around 1,000 leads a day. I've only generated 50 leads or so per day with it, but it's on autopilot. So you can go to a site like leadimpact.com and you can buy cost per view or pay per view advertising.

It's a little different from other types of advertising in that you're paying per view of your page, you're not paying per click on an ad. It's actually more like a pop up, so you're paying for these ads to pop up on people's sites, and it's run through software, so it's different than someone, say going to Google and seeing pay per click ads. You can advertise on any URL on the internet as long as the user has the software installed on their computer. So this allows you to bid on different URLs online. Now can't you see how this could be popular and profitable? Because you could bid on your competitor's URL's. You could bid on so many different URL's it's not even funny. You could bid on PPC URL's even.

So for people who are spending gobs and gobs of money on PPC, you can take those URL's that they're using for their landing pages, plug it into lead impact and then be bidding for ad space for those URLs through the software. One place to learn more about PPV and CPV is cpvden.com. It can be a nice little lead flow generator that's different from the other lead flow sources you might be generating leads from right now.

What you need to know about also is you can generate tons and tons of traffic for a lot less money, but the traffic won't be as responsive because they didn't click thru to your ad. Because they didn't click through to your ad it's kind of like an annoying pop up that comes in their face but it's all legal and they know they're getting pop ups in exchange for using the software that they're using.

It's an agreement they made before downloading the software that they're using on their computer. Say a company, like lead-impact.com, let's say they say, "You can use this software, which has huge value in exchange for being able to run an ad on your computer 5 times per day." So instead of charging for the software each month, they get the software for free, but they have to see ads, and this is where your ads can get in front of their face. You can get in front of millions of people for .017 cents each time your ad is shown, which is a fraction of a penny.

But like I said, with other forms of advertising you may get a high opt-in rate on your squeeze page such as 10% and on some ad sources, 10% is very good. On some ad sources, 10% is horrible. On some ad sources, like solo ads, for example 30% is very good, depending on whether they actually send your solo ad or not because 60% may be considered good on there, as well.

But with PPV advertising, we're talking 1-2% could be good, just depending on how much money you're spending, how much money you're making up front and how much money you're making on the backend. But because you can get traffic so cheap, it doesn't mean that the traffic is created equal to other advertising sources.

Because they haven't clicked through any targeted advertising, the traffic responsiveness will be lower as far as opting into your squeeze page goes.

The point is… all that matters is your ROI, not your opt-in rate… because your opt-in rate is always going to be different depending on where your traffic is coming from.

## Bartering for leads

Bartering for leads is a really great way to generate the highest quality leads you can generate besides having your own product and having an affiliate program. In actuality, it is almost the same or identical to that, except for you are NOT selling your own product. Here's how it works… What you want to do is go to a marketer who does product launches, who is bigger than you are online. They don't have to be huge; you could just go to someone who does WSO's, for example.

If you go to someone who does WSO's often, you can say this, "I'll do customer service for your launch," or "I'll write the sales page for your launch," or "I'll create bonuses for your launch," or "I'll help create the products for your launch," or "I'll help create buzz using social media for your launch," or "I'll help get JV's on board for your launch" or, "I'll do (something) for your launch in exchange for leads." So you're not asking for money, you're asking for leads.

You're not asking for them export leads to you; we're talking about just placing some kind of bonus of yours on their download page that customers have to opt-in for, which you get the lead for. For example, this one time I did one of these bartering for leads deals with a top marketer, and for his bonuses on his actual sales page, I advertised my bonuses that they're going to have to opt-in for. So on the download page there was a link to my squeeze page, which allowed them to opt-in to download the bonuses. On the page after the squeeze page was the download page for the bonuses.

I didn't send them through any kind of sales funnel, but the thing is, you get a list of red-hot buyers when you do this. I'm talking about scorching hot buyers. That first week of having that list you want to promote your highest converting thing, do a webinar or do something that you made money within the past because this is the time to sell them while they're the hottest and they're buyers (you have gained trust by them listening or watching your bonus, depending on what the product is, so they will be responsive).

Actually, the way I came up with the bonus for these kinds of launches is I would just use private label rights. So I use private label rights material that was a video course that I didn't even record, but I had rights to give away as a bonus to a paid product. So that's something to think about. One of my best tactics was solo ads, one was ad swaps, and at one point click banking. I did click banking on a big scale. Bartering for leads was a huge, huge tactic that I've done before. It's not a current phase I'm going through but it works like a charm. It's not going anywhere. It will always be effective.

It's a very simple tactic where you barter your skills with a product launcher who adds your bonus to their download page and the customers have to opt-in for it. It's not like relying on Google for leads because they can slap that away somehow for you. And it's not getting less effective like ad swaps are for example.

## Your own affiliate program

Another way to generate red-hot quality leads is by having your own affiliate program. Now I'm going to tell you that I've mainly generated leads through using Rapid Action Profits. I know that a lot of people in recent days have moved on to other scripts, such as Warriorplus.com, WSO Pro or JVZoo.

com or DigiResults.com, but I like trusty old Rapid Action Profits. It may cost $197, whereas I bought it for something like $297. It's always being updated so it's not out of date with technology or anything, but the reason why I like Rapid Action Profits over any other is two-fold.

For one, I only have to pay a fee one time to use it. So I pay my $197 for the script and I use it over and over and over. A lot of these other sites, you may not have an upfront fee, but they take out fees for every sale you make so you end up paying a lot more than you would pay with that one-time fee to RapidActionProfits.com. Or there may be, like with WSO Pro, you have to pay a fee every time you want to start a WSO with.

I'd rather have a script like Rapid Action Profits so I can use it over and over and over. This is just my personal opinion and preference. Also, I think there is a lot of wisdom in what I'm about to tell you with Rapid Action Profits vs. the other solutions.

The other solutions are like affiliate networks, so when you're recruiting affiliates to actually promote your product, they may end up promoting someone else's product, but with Rapid Action Profits, you have complete control over the situation. So once you show people your affiliate program, there's only an option to promote you. Therefore, whenever I launch a product on Rapid Action Products, at the bottom of the screen I have a link that says, "Affiliates make 100% commissions." They click there and then they sign up for my affiliate program through Rapid Action Profits.

They can now get their link and they can then sell the product. If I use the other programs, and I have a link at the bottom that says, "Sign up here to promote my product," and then they go to some affiliate network, they'll probably end up promoting some other product that they find. They may get lost in the sea of products trying to find mine; they give up and don't promote any product at all.

The best kind of affiliate program that attracts affiliates is to have an instant PayPal commission affiliate program like the ones I've been talking about. You can also use something like ClickBank, but you can't give away 100% commissions from ClickBank. With these other programs, you can give away 100% commissions, which is really attractive on the front end to affiliates, and then you can give 50% commission on the one-time offer, for example. You're making money off sales, but you are attracting affiliates that you don't have to ethically bride much to promote for you. If you're giving away 100% commissions, in my mind, you're not going to owe any other affiliates back for promoting you because you gave away 100% commissions.

Those leads that you get right away are going to be red-hot leads.

## Exit popups

Another way to add about 10% opt-in rate to any website you have is by adding an exit pop up script. You've probably seen these and they're pretty annoying. You can get one at exitsplash.com. When someone tries to leave the page, a pop up will come up that says, "Here's a quick chance to get this freebie," or whatever ad you want there. This can add 10% more opt-in rate to your page or to any website you send traffic to. Actually, depending on how aggressive you want to be, you can have multiple exit pop ups that lead to different squeeze pages.

What I've noticed in the past, doing a very aggressive launch with a marketer and bartering leads, seeing he wanted to go balls-to-the- wall, I decided that it would probably be most profitable to do a squeeze page for one offer that pops up once. If they don't take that offer, have a squeeze page that pops up for another offer. If they don't take that offer, then another squeeze will pop up for another offer. So it will be three squeeze pages popping up in a row for different offers. You will be surprised at how many leads that added onto the product launchers list.

Just think about this, the first squeeze page pops up and they get 10% opt-in rate on that; they've just got 10% of the traffic to sign up on their list. But if they don't take that, and another one pops up and they get 7% on that, well that's an extra 7% tacked on. If they don't take that one though, and they see the third squeeze page up, then maybe 5% tops into that list and all together you've got what, 22% of the people getting on your sales page or site opting into your list. That's almost as good as a decent converting squeeze page. I'll take 22% from a lot of different ad sources depending on the source.

But I will tell you this, that I believe exit pop ups are getting less effective over time because they've been used so much. It's similar to "ad blindness."

What will likely happen is that people will stop using exit pop ups and then wait a little while and then they will start using them again and they will be just as effective as they were before. That's my prediction and that happens to a lot of things where trends and tactics come and go. Tactics will work well, then they stop working as well as they have, and everyone stops using them. Then someone starts using them again and talking about how profitable it is to use it and everyone all of a sudden is using it again.

## Reverse Opt-in form

Another way to generate about 10% of your website traffic to your list on a sales page is using a reverse opt-in form. This is where someone clicks on the "Add to Cart" button or an "Order Now" button and then you have a page between your sales page and your order form. That page in between will be a Step 1 of 2 order confirmation form. So at the top it will say, "Step 1 of 2 Order

Confirmation," then they'll have to put in their email address to continue. This is a Reverse Opt-in Page.

You want to grab the email address here so that everybody who buys your product is added to your list. Also, the people who chicken out on your product, you'll have them on your list, and they can also be very high quality subscribers to have on your list. So you might find that the majority of people who actually opt into that form won't even order, but you'll end up generating a lot more subscribers from your sales page by doing that.

So you can see how all these leads will add up if you're promoting to a squeeze page or a sales page. You will see how all these leads add up by promoting to a sales page by using all the factors we're talking about here. Because if you're getting 22% opt in rates from doing exit pop ups and you're getting 10% from doing reverse opt in forms, then you are generating an extra 33% of people to your subscriber list during a launch.

That's something to think about because when you have all these affiliates hammering your page, a lot of their traffic might not want to buy the product that you have, but there will be people who buy products you are selling later on as an affiliate or as your own product.

## Buying ad space direct from webmasters

The next tactic I want to talk about is buying ad space directly from webmasters. This can be done as easily as going to different webmasters who have, say forums in your market, and asking how much it would cost to run an ad on the top of their page. First of all you're going to them and asking, "How much is your AdSense ad making you on a daily basis?" Chances are you're going to have more money to spend than they're making on this ad from AdSense.

So, say they say, "Well I'm generating 200 people to my site every day, but I'm only making $3.00 in AdSense per day." Well, if you had an ad that has a 10% click thru rate, then you can generate those people to your page for the same amount of money or more, so tell them that you want to take a test run on their page by advertising their ad in place of their Google ad.

You can pay them by PayPal and with a deal like this, "Will you run this ad one day and we'll see how much money I make," and you'll give them $5 instead of the $3.00 he makes from AdSense, for example. Then you see what happens when you run your ad on their site for that day and see how many opt ins you get, how much in sales in commissions you make from your sales funnel, and this will determine whether it's profitable or not.

If it's profitable then you can say, "Well I would like to rent that ad space from you on a monthly basis, for the rest of this month for x amount of dollars," or whatever is equivalent to $5.00 a day, or whatever you're testing. If you go to some real busy forum, for example, and you do the same thing – and if we're talking about bigger numbers here, maybe you will do a $50 test run for one day. You measure the results and see what happens and if it works out well, then what you need to do is just tell them that you want to run an ad that month for x amount of dollars. And that's traffic you don't have to touch. That's just autopilot traffic hitting your page.

You can run it on a weekly basis or anything that you can afford, but the point is these webmasters want to make more money on their sites because they're probably not making as much as you can give them using the advertising that they're running. They're making piss poor profits from AdSense, for example.

Actually, in the internet marketing space, WarriorForum. com has an option to run an ad at the top of the forum for $100 a day, and they run something like eight different spaces on there a day and yours would rotate with eight different advertisers. That's a good way to test something in the internet marketing niche.

If you want to test an ad out and see how internet marketers would respond before you go and promote something on internet marketing, then use the tactic of contacting vendors and webmasters directly and you could run a $100 ad and see what happens. Chances are you could get at least $100 clicks of traffic, or you may get 50 to 100 opt-ins. You may get one sale at $100 that makes you break even. You never know.

You never know until you try, but what I like about this media buying approach is that it's very easy traffic that you don't have to work toward, you just have to monitor your metrics.

## Nested squeeze page on a blog

Here's a tactic for generating a lot of leads from a blog. I actually built my first list of 1,000 subscribers this way in the weight loss niche before I even got into the internet market-ing niche. It's so easy. You take a blog and maybe your blog is generating 100, 200, 300 visitors per day because you're cranking content out on a daily basis. Even if you don't try to target certain keywords on your site, it's pretty easy to start generating 200 to 300 visitors per day just by cranking out content and ranking it for long tail search terms without even trying to, and actually only doing it.

Let's say your site isn't really an interactive site as much as you want it to be; it's really difficult to get a site with a lot of interactivity. Maybe your site just has a lot of traffic coming to it and doesn't really have people interacting, so it doesn't really matter if you put your squeeze page up there or not. One of the best ways to generate leads form a blog is to nest a squeeze page front and center.

Another way is by using Robert Plank's WordPress Plug-Ins. One is called Action Opt-In. This is where you can put an opt-in bar on your side bar that you go opt-in to. Once they opt-in to it, the form will disappear and say, "Thanks for subscribing," and keep the people on the blog they're on. One is Action Pop-Up, which is a fade in window that fades into your site and asks for the opt-in there in exchange for a freebie or whatever you're offering. The other is Action Comments, where if someone comments on your blog, they check a check box, and it automatically subscribes them to your list.

You can get all three, I believe, in one purchase from Robert Plank if you go to Actionoptin.com or search on Google for Action Opt- In and you'll probably find it. He's always updating that.

## Integrated cross-promotions

The next way I want to talk about generating leads is using integrated cross-promotions. I think Mark Joyner coined the term integrated marketing. Well integrated cross-promotions are different kinds of cross promos that you have with your joint venture partners other than ad swaps, click banking, or anything like JV giveaways.

These are different because these are integrated into your marketing on autopilot, so you should think about the different parts of your marketing systems that you can integrate some kind of joint venture link to.

For example, on your download page, you might have a banner that leads to one of your JV partner's squeeze pages and they have the same for you on their download page. That would be an example of an integrated cross- promotion. So instead of monetizing that part of your download page with an offer, what you'll do is do an integrated cross-promotion with one of your joint venture partners.

Another way is to cross promote your joint venture partner in your follow up series. So in your email follow up series, maybe your fifth email in the follow up series will promote their squeeze page and their fifth email in their follow up series will promote your squeeze page.

Another way is through P.S.'s of your emails that you send out. So when you're sending out an email to your list, you can make a deal with one of your joint venture partners to always promote their squeeze page in their P.S. and they have to do the same for you.

That's one way to do it. Think about the power of integrated cross- promotion. You're generating subscribers on autopilot by doing this. You can add tons per day to your list or more, all on autopilot, by doing this a set of joint venture partners or with just one, but just think about this; let's say you have 10 joint venture partners and you're going to do integrated joint venture cross-promotions with your follow up series of emails.

Say all 10 of you are in all 10 of your first follow up series emails, you all promote each other, well visitors would be flying all over the place and going onto your list if you do that.

## Viral PDF reports

The next tactic I want to talk about is using viral PDF reports. So let's say you write a little report that can be 2 to 5 pages long, as long as it's rock-solid content; it's going to be for a free report anyway, and you create a PDF report out of it. Well, inside the PDF report, you want to say that this is free to distribute.

Also inside of your PDF report, you want to have a link at the end that leads to your squeeze page or an entire ad that leads to your squeeze page. What I've found in the past is that other people started using my reports to build their lists with. So they would actually give my reports away to their squeeze pages and I would generate those subscribers under my list, the ones who actually read the report and then clicked thru at the end.

The ones who read the reports and clicked through to the end and discovered you that way, end up being some of the highest quality leads you'll get because they've just read one of your reports, and they clicked through at the end to get your freebie, and you've got them on your list.

If you're not sure how to do this, you can go to OpenOffice online. You can just type into Google, "OpenOffice" and download OpenOffice Writer. You're going to open up OpenOffice Writer and write your report. It's kind of like Microsoft Word. Then you're going to click "File" and export as a PDF. Once you do that, you have a PDF that you can give away, and you have clickable links inside the PDF and that will become your viral report. It's a little different than rebrandable reports.

If you have your own affiliate program, you can give affiliates a way to give cool content to their list and to promote you at the same time by offering a viral brandable rewritable report. This is a little bit different, a little more simplistic, and if you give enough of these reports away that are viral reports, you may see them circulating all over the place and generating leads from all over the internet.

## Affiliate list cross-promotions

The last thing I want to tell you for now about list building is using affiliate list cross-promotions. This is very simple. Let's say you have your own offer on Rapid Action Profits, and you've built an affiliate list, which is just a list of affiliates who promote your products. What you do is go to other product owners who have affiliate lists and say, "I will tell my affiliate list about your affiliate program if you do the same for yours."

You might pick up some really good affiliates like that. They might pick up a few and once you pick up affiliates, that means more traffic heading into your paid offer, which means more people on your list of high quality. This is one of those tactics that kind of makes you want to slap yourself in the head.

# Chapter 4
## PRODUCTIVITY IN A NEW BUSINESS

In this chapter we will discuss insightful tips to motivate, encourage and energize you to become a successful entrepreneur and attain your goals. Success in any aspect of your life is a result of planning out your goals and utilizing your creativity. The entrepreneurial life is a blessing and perfect personal growth opportunity that allows you the flexibility of working your professional life around your personal life instead of having to work your personal life around your professional life, as it often is when you're working for someone else.

Operating and growing as a work-from-home entrepreneur takes some serious self-discipline. While any business run from home poses some challenges, there are unique challenges that face those that are running the bulk of their business online. Taking business online is an easy concept for many people to get started with, but not always seen as a regular and devoted business. Many online entrepreneurs are trying to 'fit in' their online business into a busy life and not making the complete commitment to the business.

Although the ability to work from home provides a great deal of benefits that effect much more than just your work life, the challenges that come up can make the idea of working from home an extremely difficult endeavor. Business needs to be taken seriously to succeed. Even if you only have 10 hours a week to work your business, you need to be consistent, plan out your progress, stay focused and remember all the other parts of your life that need attention too!

Gaining the right kind of knowledge and putting that knowledge into practice will set you up for a happy and productive work life that will wonderfully mesh with your personal life. Read the following tips and advice with a determined mind that will see each idea as an opportunity to try new activities and open the door to a clearer picture of how you can use your time wisely to run an online business from the comfort of your home.

## Planning - Tips to organize your business

Being a productive entrepreneur takes a great deal of planning, but don't let this discourage you if planning and organization hasn't been your strong point. Most of the planning gets done occasionally to whenever-you-deem- it-necessary and once you learn some effective methods of planning then it will become a natural task for the operation of your business. The following tips will help in creating goals and implementing strategies to see them realized along with maintaining the motivation to keep yourself on track.

## Set short-term and long-term goals

Goal setting is effective in every area of your life. Giving yourself a clear picture of what you really want in life - in the immediate future and years down the road - is an excellent way to keep yourself motivated and energized to take action. Start the process by asking yourself:

## "What do I really want to do with my life?"

Don't allow limitations of time and money distort your answer. Just assume that there is nothing that can stop you from eventually achieving and having what you truly want.

These goals do have to be written down and kept somewhere you can look at regularly. Put your goals into concise sentences using the "SMART" system as outlined below:

**S**pecific: State exactly what you want to achieve. Can you break a larger task down into smaller items?

**M**easurable: Establish clear definitions to help you measure if you're reaching your goal.

**A**ction Oriented: Describe your goals using action verbs and outline the exact steps you will take to accomplish your goal.

**R**ealistic: Give yourself the opportunity to succeed by setting goals you'll actually accomplish. Be sure to consider obstacles you may need to overcome.

**T**ime-Bound: How much time do you have to complete the task? Decide exactly when you'll start and finish your goal.

## Brainstorm strategies to achieve your goals

Once you've defined some short-term and long-term goals, you'll want a list of possible strategies to achieve the results you're looking for. Create a list of strategy options that encompass various alternatives you could use to deliver the results you're looking for. Move beyond your comfort zone and think of any wild idea that comes to mind - you want a large list of ideas to work with. Keep this whole list to refer to in the future but pick a few ideas from the list to schedule in and add to your To Do list now.

## Strive for greatness and don't compromise

I'm sure you've heard of many stories about people achieving great success online. Perhaps you've even thought that they had something you didn't or were in a better position to start with than you. Or maybe you even discredited the story, as some marketing ploy and their 'rags to riches' story wasn't true at all. While there are a lot of schemers out there, there are also a lot of people that have genuinely focused on a goal and worked hard and smart to achieve it. You can do it too.

You can achieve whatever great things you put your mind to. When you're adding value to other people's lives, it's just a matter of making a plan, getting organized and never giving up until you can make your mark in whatever area is meant for you. Don't just settle for affiliate sales (although these sales are a nice bonus) and earning money from the success of others. That's what being an employee is all about and if you're interested in working online than you have already made the decision to be your own boss. Find your niche, explore the opportunities, and don't settle for a mediocre business that doesn't have a soul. Don't compromise on your opportunity for greatness!

## Counteract procrastination

Procrastination is one very bad habit. It affects most self-employed people from time-to-time due to the fact that there's not always someone expecting you to produce something. It's fueled by fear, lack of confidence, and dis-organization. Putting things off is a sure way to produce an ineffective business. Beat procrastination by building up new habits that make you get tasks done, like scheduling in time to do the things you've put off.

Habit breaking and making takes about 21 days to take effect, so keep this in mind as you're struggling to stop your learned habit of procrastination and creating a new habit of getting things done.

## Grow from the accountability effect

Create accountability in your work life by joining or creating a group of like- minded entrepreneurs where you share plans, ideas, and goals in weekly, bi-weekly, or monthly meetings. You can also gain this same effect with a one-on-one account-ability relationship. This type of set-up creates an inner desire to report back the results of your objectives and gives you that little extra incentive to get your plan in action. Additional benefits of being accountable to others are gaining inspiration from the insights of others, being in the position to assist others in their business focus, and developing deep and trusting relationships.

## Use the power of your mind to your benefit

The human mind is an extremely powerful tool in your business and we're not talking about intellect. The sub-conscience mind is your motivator, your dreamer, and your source of productivity. It can also be your discouragement, your criticizer, and your source of inactivity. Used properly, the power available in your mind will have an extraordinary effect on your life and your business. Keep your thoughts positive, keep them creative and, most importantly, keep away the damaging and defeating thoughts that are passed on by your environment!

## Create flexible schedules and adaptable to do lists

Unless you're the type of person that loves to stick to a specific routine and can adhere to a strict schedule, then you'll really want to cut yourself a bit of slack and create schedules and to do lists that allow for shifting of times, and deferring tasks. Working from home can involve work time getting delayed from the original plan and projects taking longer than anticipated. Just be aware of not letting work always get put on the back burner, which is very easy to do in a home office. Working from home does allow for a different approach to planning and scheduling.

When creating a schedule for a day, week, or month in advance (whatever is the best process for you) don't schedule the whole day hour for hour. For example, plan for marketing tasks Monday morning, website maintenance Tuesday afternoon, social media tasks Thursday evening, etc. Plan the time you have to conduct business, block it out for the morning, afternoon, or evening instead of 9-11am.

## Use online resources to create a schedule

It only seems appropriate that your online business should use online resources. This is effective, as you can keep focused on what you need to do with a click into a browser instead of switching your focus to paper, another program or another device. This is also great for anybody that happens to use more than one computer or device for their work as you can quickly access your schedule, as long as you've got an internet connection, which is necessary for your business anyway.

Google Calendar is a great option for this. You can sync Google Calendar with an iPhone or Android device and set it up to notify you in different ways of upcoming entries in your schedule. Create a strict or casual schedule - whatever you feel is best for you - and if you tend to like the paper approach you can print off your schedule as well. As with most Google products, it's quite customizable to your preferences.

## Use online resources to create a to do list

All the little jobs that you want to do or need to get done should be written down on a list. This list will be comprised of thoughts and ideas that pop into your head; tasks to do to move toward your goals and regular tasks that you need to do in the operation of your business. Using an online program for this has the same benefits as using an online calendar.

Trello is a flexible and user-friendly option for organizing your ideas and projects in one area. You can create many boards and different organizations, which is very helpful when you want to start a new project in your business. A board consists of a 3-column listing of "To Do" "Doing" and "Done" (which you can change the names of), and you can add in comments, checklists, due dates, files and customize to your liking in several different ways. You can also share a Board or Organization with other people, so you can collaborate with others on a project and see what's been done, who has done it and what needs to be done. It's also beneficial to share your task list with someone that can simply check up on your progress to add that bit of accountability motivation.

## Make it official and make a business plan

Many home businesses never get the benefit of a well thought out approach to operations and expectations. Although business plans are especially popular for those who are in search or financing, every person that would like to make money with their business should have spent the time creating some type of business plan. You don't need to focus on the financial details as much as a traditional plan would, but you want to create a plan of how your business will operate and what the products and/or services are. A business plan makes you think about various parts of running a business and clarifies its viability in the marketplace. It may also force you to think of a more viable business venture if your original idea does not look as good written down as it did in your head. The Internet is full of great resources to assist you in creating an effective business plan.

## See each day as a fresh start to your business

Don't let any setbacks from yesterday or any point in the past allow you to judge your effectiveness for today. Only focus on what did work and what has been going well for you so far and leave all the negative stuff behind you. Each day will have a new plan of attack that you use to your advantage in building your business. Frustration and defeating thoughts are BIG productivity stealers and have no place in growth of a business.

## Create a small routine to get you "in the mood" to work

If you were leaving home to go to work, you would have a transition period of getting ready for work at home and traveling to a location and then settling into your workspace. When working within your home, you need to create some type of routine that becomes a sub-conscience signal for your brain to get focused on work. As an example, you might prepare yourself a drink (coffee, tea, smoothie), bring it into your work area, turn on some non- vocal music, then read a book on personal and/or professional development for 15 minutes.

## Make a today list

Similar to a To Do List, a Today List is an informal yet intentional way of thinking about what you want to accomplish in your day. Get yourself a pad of sticky notes of whatever size you would like to be able write down daily tasks. You may want to consult a 'master' To Do list or some type of schedule that you have created to be aware of what your overall tasks are. Write down short, to the point notes of what you plan to accomplish in your day then stick this somewhere where you can easily glance at it throughout the day.

You can add to this list as the day goes on as you might think of a phone call you need to make or new task that comes up. The most important part of this exercise is the conscience thinking about your day and writing down your intentions as you begin working. This little list should get chucked at the end of the day and don't make any judgments on yourself about whether you did what you had planned to at the beginning of the day or not. Start a new list at the beginning of a new working day. If there are tasks that you want to remember to do that didn't get done from your Today List, then just transfer them to your schedule or business To Do List.

## Do the small but essential tasks first

Attending to email, making phone calls, or updating your social media accounts may be possible essentials that need daily attention.

They are also things that can be distracting if you are returning to them throughout your working time. This is why it is effective to do these jobs to begin with and possibly to finish off with as well. You will likely have other responsibilities that fit into this category, depending on the type of business you run - think of all those little things you do that take focus away from other jobs.

## Don't get caught up on getting everything perfect

Many precious hours can be wasted on spending too much time perfecting something. Although you want to portray a certain level of professionalism, don't be overly concerned with getting the perfect look, the perfect words, or the perfect plan. You can always add something on your To Do list if you're not really satisfied with how it initially worked out. This allows you to at least complete the task at hand and move on to other productive tasks.

## Effectiveness: Tips to getting results!

To be productive you must approach your business with a specific mindset that is relaxed, determined and open. It is most helpful to create processes and delegate when needed and keep focused on the task at hand while avoiding distractions that take that focus away. Being effective at everything you do and with the thinking you do is a major contributor to a productive and prosperous business. Use these following ideas to get the most out of your workday.

## Keep your desktop free of clutter

At the end of office time for the day put everything in its place, which can be a combination of drawer's shelves, wall files, filing cabinets and any other organizing elements you are utilizing. Clutter in your environment, clutters your mind and can lead to inefficient practices from disorganization. Keep this great little saying in mind: "Everything has its place and there's a place for everything. If there's not a place for it then you don't need it!"

## Create a space to put papers that you need to deal with eventually

This may be a box (sized slightly larger than standard letter sized paper and 3-4 inches in height) on your desk, a set of stackable organizer inboxes, or a multi-pocket/single pocket wall file (great for freeing up desktop space.) Unless you feel that you need the separation, don't create one space for work and one for home. Consider this a one-stop drop for anything you can deal with later and schedule a regular time that you attend to these papers. Don't let it pile too high so that you feel daunted by the effort to go through it.

## Create systems for your business

The most efficiently run businesses are made up of a regulated and unique group of tasks that are created once and repeated again and again and again. If you've been in business for any length of time you probably have a few systems in place already, even if you don't realize it. Make the time to write down a step-by-step guide to the mechanics of your business; what you do in your home office that affects your business. This process will not only help you in defining and organizing the tasks you do (or should do) as an entrepreneur but will also allow you to have someone else keep your business running if you're unavailable for various reasons, which moves us on to the next tip.

## Outsource business tasks that you don't need to personally do

Every entrepreneur has "stuff" to do that isn't part of their skill set and isn't enjoyable to them. Generally, finances don't allow them to pay others for essential business tasks, especially when starting up, yet many people will find that as soon as they offload those unappealing chores, they become more efficient at other jobs and their business really starts to flourish. In our multi-communication society, outsourcing business projects is easier than ever and definitely has various benefits to hiring an employee. You can find freelance professionals that are eager to do any project you may have through a variety of avenues. Whether you post a job on one of the many freelance bidding sites (Upwork and Freelancer, to name a few), search for a virtual assistant online or through your local resources, or just have a friend or family member complete some work, you can put yourself in a position to achieve more with less time.

## Pay attention to business tasks during your business time

This may seem like it's an opposite of being productive. After all, with our technology at the level that it is we can have the devices and access to our business 24/7. And why not attend to a few emails or phone calls if time permits during non-business hours? First of all, because those business matters won't really have your full attention if you're out shopping or visiting with friends, and secondly, just as you should give your business your full attention, you should also give the other areas of your life your full attention.

This advice may not be for everyone, but perhaps it's just something for you to think about for now.

## Be devoted to just one project at a time

Whether it is work or personal, remove all other programs and browsers that aren't related to what you're working on. As well, clear your desk/ working space of anything that is not related to the task at hand.

## Set boundaries of when you answer emails and telephone calls

Keep in mind that these various forms of communication are for your convenience and not for the convenience of others. You can't be as focused and efficient when you're letting distractions always take you away from the task at hand. Schedule in a period of time once or twice a day to respond to and initiate conversations, whether it be through email, texting, phone calls or any other form of communication with customers, business associates and personal contacts.

## Use the Pomodoro technique

This technique was created in the 1980's by Francesco Cirillo, which assists in achieving greater focus and better time management. It's a fairly simple concept of breaking down your workday into blocks of 25 minutes and builds on that main practice to teach more in-depth techniques of blocking out distractions, accurately estimating the length of time to do a task, and other organizational tips. You may not want to be a true 'Pomodoro' follower but reading the details about this technique will definitely provide you with some insightful ideas to better manage your home business.

## Schedule closed-door and quiet periods of time

While it can be good to be accessible to family members if needed, you may need to make at least a couple of 'no interruptions' times in your week. Some tasks just need your full-uninterrupted attention and if you can do them without any chance of an interruption, then you will be able to produce much better results. Not everyone will need to use this tactic, but if you find that you're less productive due to minor interruptions then stand-up for yourself and your business and make your family aware of the times you have set aside to complete your high concentration tasks that may also mean a quieter time for everyone in the house.

## Do productivity checks

This will be a great new habit to foster that will help to keep you focused and stopping lots of those time-wasting activities. Every hour or two check in with yourself asking "Is this the best use of my time?" Set an alarm to go off, set up Google Calendar to send a notification to your desktop or simply stick a note on the wall in your direct sight with this question on it. Eventually you will get in the habit of asking this question regularly without external prompts and not get into unproductive work to begin with.

## Don't get lost in multi-tasking

Creating an environment that is extremely efficient involves a sustained time of focused work. It can be difficult to really get focused when, each day, you're switching from one activity to another, just to get things done. Being able to schedule your time so that you complete a months' worth of blog posts in one day or set up some email broadcasts for the next two weeks allows your brain to really get into the one project and produce better work in less time than if you broke up the same kind of job over several days.

## Always generate a growing sense of optimism

Expect that good things are going to be plentiful. Have the sense that life will bring good rather than bad outcomes and that when you encounter less than ideal situations you will be able to overcome it. Living your life with an optimistic mindset will allow you to see the possibilities and take advantage of opportunities that come out of hardship.

## Create your business around your passion

The most successful people have attested to the fact that their passion for their business drove them to be innovative, determined and keep focused on their tasks. Be sure that your business focus is somehow connected to something you're passionate about and you'll find that staying motivated and productive feels much easier.

## Schedule your more challenging work during your prime time

Are you a morning person, or does your energy rev up after 6pm? Determine when you are at your peak performance and schedule the more difficult work, or the stuff you are not so keen on doing, during these times. The routine tasks and more enjoyed activities can then be scheduled for the other times of the day

## Incorporate a reward system for a job well done

Although you've got "the big picture" incentive of having an awesome online business for long-term motivation, it's useful to create some short- term incentives to help you get through a challenging undertaking or detailed project. Gear the incentive to your own preference of what you see as a reward.

## Balance – Tips to Energize Your Work Life!

Use the following tips and advice to create a better-rounded life. Working from home affords you the luxury of taking longer breaks, creating a unique home life and fulfilling your desires related to every part of your life while running a successful business. Your life goal should be to have a prosperous life, and although this can mean financial prosperity, it more importantly points to prosperity in all areas of your life that will result in an increase in your enthusiasm for your business. Strive for balance and creating harmony between work and life. The following tips focus on creating balance in your life that will directly influence your business.

## Always be learning and growing

Always have a book on the go. Reading is a vital component to self- development, which you should be making time for on a regular basis. This is to enrich both your personal development and your professional development. Just making time to fit 15 minutes of reading in will benefit you greatly in all areas of your life, which will directly result in better results in your business.

## Schedule your time for business matters, don't impose on your personal time

Don't let all the "to dos" get in the way of your personal life. Working from home can end up with some people working all the time, which sort of defeats the purpose of being self-employed. Make that schedule for business tasks and work within that schedule. There can be the occasional exceptions of course, but when you find that you're not sticking to the flexible schedule that you had created, you either need to re-think your time or be more disciplined in your approach to working time.

## Don't aim to please everyone

Be clear on what your motives and intentions are and don't let someone else's opinion sway your informed decision. This relates to people in your personal life and in your business. Whether it's customers that want more time from you or quicker responses, or a spouse that feels your online pursuits are taking up too much time or doesn't understand your passion, don't let the opinions of others change your business process when you know that's what you want. Don't be completely close-minded either. Hear people out and consider their opinion, then stand up for what you feel is right.

## Share your work schedule with your family

Posting a printout of your weekly schedule on the fridge, office door or other visible area will let your family members know when you have planned to work and even what kind of work you'll be doing. This helps to avoid someone in your house planning something that requires or requests your involvement during your work hours and allows you to share a bit of your business life with your family.

## Discuss your business challenges and accomplishments with family and friends

Have one or two people that you can regularly talk to about what's happening with your business. Especially when you're first starting out, it can be discouraging to feel like you don't have anyone to share the achievements and the frustrations with. Even though you can connect with many other people online in the same situation as you (which you should do) it's much more effective to get to vent and share with someone you already have an established relationship with.

## Take at least a 15-minute break for every 2 hours of work

When you're mainly focusing on your computer screen, you can get fatigued much more quickly than if you are moving around. After sitting at your computer for 2 hours, get up and get a drink, have a stretch, take a walk, anything that gets you on your feet and not staring at a screen. You'll find yourself more focused and refreshed after a short break.

## Use the freedom of your work-from-home lifestyle to have getaway breaks

If you're working a number of hours in your home business, then take breaks where you can possibly do some personal errands or leave the house for an hour or two to take in some physical activity or meet up with someone. Shifting your focus for a longer length of time and creating a day that is filled with a variety of activities provides a greater feeling of satisfaction with your day, as you've been able to give attention to several areas of your life.

## Take a reading break

If you haven't made the time in any other part of your day to devote to your personal growth through reading, then take a reading break. Find yourself a comfortable spot to lounge in, go outside if possible or just locate yourself in a different spot than where you were working. It's good to get a change of scenery and fit in the always- important element of learning.

## Use your work break to give attention to the other areas of your life

The most effective kind of break to take is a break that has you giving attention to some other areas of your life. Using your time wisely in this way will create a more productive life and not just center on a more productive work life. As the points above described more specific things you can do with your essential break, it is important to keep in mind that making your work break a short and sweet time to see family or a lengthy outing to experience various other things is an integral aspect to creating a balanced life that will have a direct result on the productivity in your business.

## Be nutritionally conscience

Eating right is essential on so many levels, but you will find you are so much more motivated and productive if you're feeding your body the right kind of fuel. Get educated on what the best diet is for you and eat a variety of foods that are providing your body with the appropriate nutrients that it needs to function at an optimum level.

Try to eat with the focus that food is for the proper functioning of your body and not just for your taste buds. Of course, moderation is the key and having little treats now and then is acceptable but make the majority of meals and snacks about providing your body the right fuel.

## Engage in fun and rejuvenating physical activity

Physical activity is a great energizer and provides your whole body with overall feeling of satisfaction. Although any type of exercise is beneficial, it is an added bonus when you can get some exercise while having fun and possibly spending some quality time with family or friends. A few examples of this type of invigorating exercise are biking, brisk walking, playing sports, skipping, jumping on a trampoline, and rock climbing, just to name a few of your options. Even if you just take a regular trip to the gym and give your body a workout, you'll reap the rewards of physical activity. The overall point here is that exercise can and should be integrated into your life and it doesn't have to be some rigorous workout in the gym. There's a whole world of possibilities.

## Nourish your spiritual side

You are a spiritual being that needs to regularly nourish that aspect of yourself. If you don't feel drawn to an organized faith or religion, just be connected to the spiritual nourishment of nature. Realize that there is more to life than just what you see and think about and take time every day to become aware of your inner spirit through mediation, communing with nature, or learning about various spiritual aspects of humanity.

## Make time for face-to-face socialization

Get connected face-to-face with people in all aspects of your life, whether they are family, friends, business associates or casual acquaintances. Try to make brief encounters and lengthy visits a chance to really connect with someone and not just a passing of time. You never know what may come of a conversation where you are truly in the moment and making the most of your time with someone.

## Schedule in time to nurture the most important relationships

Just being around your spouse or your children, or any other vital people in your life, isn't going to be an effective way to value that relationship. You have to spend quality time with the people you love, and this is easily left out if you're not aware of the lack of connection you may have. If you find you're not connecting with those special people in your life on an intimate level, then schedule in a weekly 'date' where you spend time with one another and get a chance to openly talk.

## Be an ongoing source of inspiration for others

Being an encouragement to other people to have great aspirations, be persistent in achieving their goals and being open to new opportunities creates a greater sense of ownership in all you are planning to achieve in your business and personal life. Keep the momentum by reaching out to other people that you know personally and that you connect with through online sources. When you are constantly inspiring others you will be building a habit of determination and success that will lead you to living your life to its fullest potential.

## Live the life of a successful online entrepreneur!

Surround yourself with empowering messages and people and avoid negative voices and mediocre minds. All the challenges that are faced by those working their business from home are eventually overcome by getting rid of those ineffective habits and renewing their life with a set of new productive habits that are the building blocks to a successful and well- balanced life. Building an online business is an achievable feat for anyone - you don't need to start off with special skills or have a lot of money in the bank and you don't need to have everything figured out. Learn as you go and be open to change, especially the change that needs to take place in your mind to think and execute plans like a determined entrepreneur.

Take risks and try new things that have the potential to get you in a position of growth and wisdom. Gain knowledge wherever and whenever you can to keep motivated and informed. Planning out various aspects of your business, being effective in your approach and having a life that is balanced in all areas will provide you a clear path to complete life of fulfillment.

Don't count on the success of your business niche, count on the success of you. If you focus the right attention and determined attitude to keep at it and don't get stuck in a rut or a process that doesn't work, then you'll always be able to roll with the punches and keep on keeping on.

# Chapter 5
## Becoming the Leading Authority

One of the most important things you can do for your online business is to become an authority in your market. People underestimate the value of a recognized brand, but when they finally take action and begin building authority in their market, they are shocked by how much it impacts their business.

When you have secured authority in your market, you will:

- Generate unlimited traffic to your site

- Drive conversion rates through the roof

- Gain access to endless joint venture opportunities

- Increase prices for all your products

- Grow a massive, targeted mailing list

- Command attention and recognition.

Authority equates to more money, because when people recognize you as a leader in your market, there is very little resistance when purchasing your products and services.

Since you have more at stake (your reputation and credibility), even new customers who research you feel far more comfortable buying from someone that other people recommend, and trust. So, how can you quickly become an authority in your market and outsell the competition? This chapter outlines 7 power steps to becoming a trusted authority in your market, by building a world class brand, all your own.

## Complete market domination

Building a brand and becoming a leader in your market isn't nearly as difficult as you may think, but it involves a very strict focus. Rather than trying to be everything to everyone, you need to begin with one market at a time. You then work towards complete market domination by saturating the market with YOUR brand. To do this, you will need to first choose your niche. Consider this carefully because when you tie your brand to one topic or market, you will forever be linked as an authority in that specific field.

Consider:

- What are you experienced with?

- What are you most interested in?

- What do you feel you can offer that's unique and valuable?

- What do you want to be known for?

Once you have chosen your niche, it's time to begin a full market assault. You will need to set up a website, squeeze page and social media accounts to begin weaving your brand message throughout your industry. While this can take a bit of time, once you have the brand-building tools in place, it will be easy to replicate for other niche markets.

Your website is key to building your brand and authority. You can set it up a number of different ways, including by using WordPress as the foundation for your entire network. Just make sure that you optimize it based on your audience, and offer high quality content, tools, and resources.

Here's our top recommended resource for help in building a full featured WordPress blog wpunraveled.com. Part of building authority in your market requires going above and beyond what other marketers in your field are doing. You want to stand out and offer your audience genuinely helpful information and tools that showcase your commitment to providing value. Regardless of the niche market you are involved in, your brand begins with offering tremendous value. You will quickly become the "go to" person in your market if you give more than your competitor's give, and you are transparent with your intentions to help your audience, nurture relationships with your customers, and provide exceptional value throughout every campaign, beginning with your website. When adding content to your website, consider outsourcing to professionals so that you're able to deliver the best quality material possible.

Consider creating "pillar content" within your authority-building campaigns. Pillar content forms the foundation for your website and is considered your very best material. Pillar content is usually in the form of tutorials, step-by-step lessons, guides and "how to" based products and offers long-term appeal. You should accompany this with downloadable material where visitors can opt into your mailing list in order to receive free products and information. Always be on the lookout for ways to build authority by developing your very own mailing list!

Just keep in mind that the quality of your content is the driving force behind being able to create a brand recognized for value and authority. Your objective is to become an expert in your market, and so everything you do needs to emphasis your ability to deliver solid, high-quality content.

## Siphon credibility from authority figures

One of the easiest ways of building authority in your market is to siphon credibility from established leaders. They have already done the hard work in building relationships with their peers and customers, and in solidifying their place in your niche, so by associating yourself to them, you can siphon instant authority that will go towards building your own brand! You can begin by targeting 5-10 leaders in your market, paying close attention to any outlet in which you can become visibly active.

For example, one easy way of siphoning credibility is to begin communicating with their audience through forums, websites, and blogs. Leave valuable feedback including tips that will help their visitors, and through direct association and by providing value, you'll be able to garner attention instantly! Another powerful technique is to interview the experts, and then offer this as a unique product on your own website! By interviewing experts, not only are you able to develop a unique, high-quality product absolutely free (and very quickly), but you are able to associate yourself with the authority in your market!

People love interviews, because it gives them insight into how an authority thinks, what they've done to be successful and what your audience can do to achieve the same success.

## Trade content for credibility

Another easy way of building authority in your market by borrowing credibility by association is to become a guest blogger. You can submit quality content that features your website links for distribution amongst authority blogs and websites.

Marketers and authority figures are always on the lookout for quality content that they can publish on their website. Their objective is to cater to their audience, while minimizing their workload and so by offering to guest write on their site, you both win!

You can also submit your content into content syndication networks and outlets that will circulate your articles throughout some of the leading websites and communities in your niche market. Run a quick search for content syndication channels in your niche, and then begin contacting all of the top leaders. Make sure that you have at least 2-3 high-quality, full-length articles to submit and that they are 100% unique. Authority blogs and websites do not want to post rehashed content or material that can be found anywhere else, so you need to be sure that your content provides exceptional value!

## Create your own product line

You can also piggyback off of the success of authorities in your market by creating auxiliary products and special offers around THEIR products. For example, choose 2-3 leaders in your field and identify what it is that they are offering their customers. Analyze their websites and products and then create your very own special offer around their main product. Do NOT copy their product, but instead, create an offer that ties into their brand, and offers additional value to customers. Then, give it away on your website.

Not only will you be able to generate traffic quickly, but you can offer the download through the back end of your mailing list, so you can build a massive list of your own.

Then, take it a step further by creating additional products that you can sell to your new audience. The objective is to swipe traffic and credibility from leading authorities, and then turn that traffic into your very own customer base. You will do this faster and easier when you're able to offer a full product line of your own. Start by developing a single product, and then expand your sales system to include one-time offers and back-end products. If you need to outsource the creation of your product, consider the following resources:

WarriorForum.com (especially valuable for finding writers, designers, and copywriters).

Guru.com (great place for expert writers) Fiverr.com (great place for cheap content that you can use to build your list – blog posts, articles, etc.)

Note: You can use high-quality private-label content as bonus products and value enhancers, from places like QuickStartPLR.com however your primary products should all be original and exclusive to your brand.

## Brand yourself

From day one, every marketing campaign, website, and product that you create should carry your brand messaging, identifying yourself as an authority in your market.

Create a signature for use on all blogs, websites, and forums that you participate in and include direct links to all platforms that you are a part of including:

- Your money pages (sales pages)

- Websites

- Blogs

- Hubs

- Social Media Accounts

- Articles

- Syndicated Content

You want to saturate your name and URL everywhere you can so that people begin to recognize it. Include a sign off in every email, every forum, and on every social media site that you participate in. Forums are a great vehicle for building your brand and generating mass exposure for free, so search out the top 2-3 forums in your niche and get active!

## Link your offers to established products

Another simple way of siphoning authority from existing leaders is to write comprehensive, full-scale reviews of their products. At the end of your review, offer a free resource that ties into the core product, and offers extended value. For example, if an authority in your market is selling a guide to making money with WordPress, you could write up a review outlining the key benefits of purchasing their product, while also offering a free set of WordPress themes that will help customers minimize their workload.

Not only will you make money from promoting the product as an affiliate, but you will gain authority and recognition by offering a quality bonus for free! You can begin building your website on WordPress, instantly. Not only will this save you time, but WordPress is absolutely free. Once you have created your website and developed (or outsource) expert written content, you will want to implement affiliate links, a shopping cart for your own products as well as thank you pages and more. You can do all of this easily with WPSalesBuddy. com a robust WordPress based plugin that will instantly create secure download pages, subscription links, shopping cart links and more.

## Build a membership site

Nothing speaks of authority as a membership site does! When you build a subscription-based website, not only are you able to secure your place in your market faster, but you'll be able to generate a passive, recurring income from your niche market.

Nearly every authority figure offers a membership program of some kind because it's the most powerful way of building relationships in your market and securing your foothold as a leader in your field. Membership sites go beyond just the exchange of information and resources. Your membership site can easily become a full-scale community, where you are recognized as the leader instantly, while being able to tap into an ever-growing customer base that can ultimately maximize your profits faster than anything else.

Start off with a simple membership program that offers monthly content, tools and resources and then expand your outreach by creating upgrades and additional products that tie into your membership theme. The easiest way to build a dynamic, full featured membership program while also building your list, offering unlimited one time offers, back-end products and more is through ClickFunnels, the leader in membership software. You can find out more at clickfunnels.com

## Final tips

Building authority in your market will dramatically increase your overall income, while setting you up for long-term success. Once you've established authority in your market, it's extremely easy to dominate nearly any niche just by spreading your authority throughout. Here is to dominating your market and maximizing your income for life!

# Chapter 6
## Outsourcing in Your Business

If you're a business owner, you already know how burden-some and stressful it can seem to get everything you want accomplished on many rushed and hurried days. For Internet business owners, they may find themselves over their heads at times when it comes to getting everything they need for their business completed in a timely fashion.

Today's Internet business owners are a diverse bunch; however, many of them are one-person operations—that is, there is no "staff" or "employees" to speak of. This is where outsourcing some of the work that needs to be done can really come in handy—and provide you with more free time to get other things done. Outsourcing simply means that you delegate various work and tasks to other people for a set amount of pay, usually in the form of a one-time payment.

Since business online is booming, the need for more quality people to assist business owners with various tasks is stronger than ever. It can be hard to find good people you can trust to get the job done. In fact, today over half of all Internet businesses use the services from outsourcing resources and websites to help them accomplish their business goals. There are many significant benefits to outsourcing work.

Perhaps the most obvious one is the low and fair cost. You can outsource work to others on a case-by-case basis, so you are only paying for the satisfactory completion of very specific assignments. This is much more cost effective than if you were to hire a full-time staff of employees. Staff requires salaries or hourly pay plus benefits, not to mention the overhead of a building to keep them all in.

Outsourcing work can come from all over the world, and you can find eligible candidates through a large number of different helpful websites. Most people who perform freelance work are familiar with the client's needs and the pay rate, so don't be afraid to be very vocal about what you want done, and what you are willing to pay for it. This new modern method of getting help from outside sources is a great way to network. In addition, it is a real time saver that is often worth its weight in gold.

You may wonder just what type of work can be done through outsourcing. Some of the most common tasks include graphic design, web page design, script writing (web), content writing, editing, copywriting, coding, software creation, ebooks, and even customized music for your website.

The possibilities are limitless today. If you only need one logo created for your website, for example, you can enlist the help of a freelance graphic artist and then pay him or her a one-time fee for the logo. It makes running a virtual business that much easier.

Remember, when looking for someone to do a job for your business, be sure to ask for some kind of credentials, like a portfolio or a reference. Think of it as doing an interview via email for a new employee. You don't want to pay someone simply because they SAY they can do the job.

If you enter into some kind of payment agreement and then you're not happy with their work, you may be in a legal bind, so be certain the person you choose to do the assignment is qualified and able to produce what you are looking for.

Outsourcing has increased almost exponentially over the last few years. This means as a business owner, the resources for finding great talent have increased as well. You can use several different websites to "recruit" the help you need. In some cases, all you need to do is post the need for the job, a thorough job description of what needs to be done, and a price you're willing to pay for it upon completion.

People then bid on the job and submit your qualifications, and you can decide who you'd like to "hire" by either the price they bid or the background information they provide. A great advantage to using these types of sites is that in many cases the website will guarantee you're happy with the job before you pay. This ensures that you get exactly what you need without incurring any extra costs.

Time is so precious to so many business owners, it is no wonder more and more of them are looking to outsource various tasks. It is also much less expensive than hiring someone to work for them full time. You can choose the job you need done and how soon you need it completed.

Outsourcing also gives you the freedom you need to make a budget for each task. How much or how little you are willing to pay is completely up to you, and then those who are interested in doing the job will contact you through either direct email or through the post you create on a number of outsourcing websites. You can control how much money you're willing to spend, which gives you great flexibility.

## Outsourcing as an investment

If you own an Internet business, surely you know there are many costs involved. Aside from the common cost of web hosting, domains and company email addresses, there are many other expenditures you need to consider. Even with an online business, you need to be as professional as possible. Business cards are great for networking when attending conferences or meeting people face to face.

You also need to consider the cost of faxes, copies (as well as printer ink), a cell phone and service, and a land line if you need one. Don't forget the smaller costs of pens and other office supplies. As far as larger costs go, you can incur anything from inventory to shipping costs, as well as the price of providing whatever service it is you are offering your customers and clients.

With all of these costs to consider, outsourcing may initially look like just another mark on your general ledger. Keep in mind that when you use outsourcing, in most cases you will only need to pay for the services you receive on an individual basis. Most people who run traditional brick-and- mortar businesses typically have much more financial overhead. They must pay for a building to lease or buy, utility bills, phone book listings, as well as the salary they must pay their employees. With outsourcing, this overhead can be cut significantly.

Outsourcing should be looked at as more of an investment versus an overhead cost. This is because the services you use will be something that your business can keep forever. For example, if you're selling ebooks, having one person write an ebook for you at a one-time price can bring you a lifetime of residual income. A graphic designer will usually take a flat fee per design, while your logo sticks with the business for life, and provides you with branding. People who provide content for your website are giving you text that people will read and see on your website for as long as you wish to keep it there.

Of course, the best thing about outsourcing is the fact that you will have much more time to focus on other aspects of your business. As they say, time is money and the more time you have to attend meetings, procure more inventory, and focus on marketing, the more money you'll generate. With the help of outsourcing, you are investing in your business. You can take more time to actually get the things done you need to do without worrying about where the extra help will come from. In today's web-based world, the resources to find reliable people for outsourcing is quite expansive.

Some of your associates or competitors might initially scoff at the idea of outsourcing, but in the long run they'll be literally amazed at how much time and money you have saved. You will get projects and issues with your website completed while freeing up time to get other things done.

Those who scoff might still be running around worried about how they are going to get everything accomplished for the day so that their business can progress. Be proud of the fact that you're finding and using an extremely valuable resource that will give you back much more than just finished jobs. Outsourcing provides you with peace of mind and another tick on your checklist.

You should view outsourcing as an investment, since it will save you time and money, and will provide your business with the things you need in order to be successful. Think of every job you pay for as another item done on your to do list, and you can feel more relaxed knowing you've put the work needed into capable hands. It is not so much something you have simply spent money on, but instead something that will bring you a return on your investment.

## The best places to outsource

The Web offers many different places to find good outsourcing assistance. Here are a few of the most commonly used websites and some of the feature they offer, so you can make an informed decision about where to find good people and resources for outsourcing work:

1. scriptlance.com This website allows you to post a number of different jobs for outsourcing. Some of the categories include web design, graphic design, SEO writing, content writing, tool development for your website, and even administrative support as it is needed.

   You can post the job type and exactly what you need, and eligible bidders can then bid on your job. It is up to you to decide whom you'd like to choose to complete the job, and then you may give them allotted time fame for completion. You may post your budget as well, so that bidders know how much you're willing to pay for a completed task.

2. rentacoder.com The website does exactly what the name says: it allows you to "rent" a coder to help you with the development of your website. This site only allows qualified web coders to apply and bid on jobs, so you can be sure you're getting high quality work. The coders are notified of new jobs posted, so the task goes out to thousands of people at one time. The bidders do not get paid until you approve the work,

which provides a great motivating factor. If you run into problems, Rentacoder has a staff of people who can assist you with either getting in touch with the coder you've chosen or help you moderate issues if a problem arises.

3. upwork.com This site is extremely thorough, and it allows all of its freelancers to take a wide variety of skills tests. These tests can vary from typing speed to grammar, web coding to office terminology fluency and comprehension. Each test that a user passes is then added to their score, so that business owners can see how well each person did on specific tests.

This is a great way to gauge how well someone will be able to complete a task for you, and a good resource for finding high quality work. Upwork allows you to post your needed project in a kind of bulletin board style, where all users can see it by category, and then bid on the job.

The site has helpful forums, video tutorials, and is registered with Verisign and the Better Business Bureau, so you know your investment is protected, and that you will receive quality work from elance members.

4. sitepoint.com This website provides a wide range of helpful information for Internet business owners. It has many great features including helpful forums and articles. There are also helpful tips for business owners in regard to marketing your website, and how to get more people to see your website. It is an invaluable resource for both you and those looking to outsource their talents.

## A list of what you can outsource

People often think of outsourcing jobs as moving a call center to India or shipping manufacturing jobs overseas. But the term outsourcing can also simply mean using someone else's help to get a job accomplished and completed. Here is a list of different things you can outsource simply by finding qualified people online:

- Ebooks

- SEO Content

- Music Composition

- Graphic design and logo design

- Web content

- Website programming and coding

- Web tool development

- Chat room and forums moderators and monitors

- Live Help assistants

- Schedule maintenance

- Virtual assistants/secretaries

- Report writing

- Telephone help

- Copywriting and editing

- Publishing assistance

- eBay listings

- Article compositions and rewrites

- Legal assistance

- Court document research

- Photography

These are just a few examples of the many different jobs you can find online through outsourcing resources. There are thousands of qualified people who actually make their living freelancing on the web. With the help of outsourcing sites, you can connect with high quality people who can provide you and your business with the essentials it needs to succeed.

Just because you own a business does not necessarily mean you can do it all yourself. Sometimes help is needed with certain tasks, and this is where outsourcing comes in. Through networking, many people often find a reliable source for outsourcing and a great person who eventually can provide them with the help they need on an assignment basis, without having to pay them an annual salary.

Brainstorm and come up with a comprehensive list of different things you will need to outsource. Think about your budget ahead of time and allot a proper amount to each task. Remember that this is an investment, and that high quality work will definitely pay for itself. You don't want to pay for too many tasks at once, so prioritize your needs and decide which things you need accomplished, and how soon. Just about anything you can think of can be outsourced. It's all a matter of properly wording the job you need done, so that people know exactly what you're looking for. Try and list one job at a time and see how it turns out. Use each website for one different job, just so you can get a feel for their fees and layout, and for what kind of quality people they are providing.

If you feel overwhelmed, just determine which task needs to be completed the soonest. Then, decide on how you want to post the listing. Wait for qualified bidders to contact you, and then make a decision on which you would like to complete it. Remember that they must adhere to the time frame that you set, and that the work must be to your liking before you pay for it.

You can always ask the person to make changed and edit things as needed, until it meets your requirements. Most people are more than happy to adjust their work to give you what you need so that they can get paid, so do not be afraid to ask them to make changes until you get exactly what you want. Remember, it is your money and your business, so you deserve the best. What to Look for in a Freelancer, Ghostwriter, Designer, etc.

If you're new to outsourcing, you want to be sure you choose someone to complete the job that is qualified. There are several things you need to look for in this type of person, since you cannot make a face-to-face connection with them, and almost all of your communication with be via email or on the web. The first thing you can do is ask the person to provide you with a portfolio.

For example, if you're in need of a graphic designer, have him or her send you some examples of the work they have done in the past for other companies. Another option is to give them a "test" example that has a quick turnaround time. This will allow them to prove to you their capabilities, as well as their ability to meet deadlines. How quick they respond also shows you how serious they are about assisting you, and how eager they are to do a good job.

For freelance writers you can ask someone to provide you with a few writing samples. Writing samples give you good insight into how well a person expresses themself. Read over the sample articles carefully so you can get a feel for how this person writes. If you feel like their style matches what you're looking for, then odds are they will do a good job writing your web content or your SEO content that you need.

If you feel so inclined, you can also ask the person for references. Many people who freelance have been doing so for some time and have probably built up a list of clients who can vouch for their work. References are a great way to ensure you're getting someone who can do the job well.

If you are searching for freelance web coders, ask for a few examples of some sites they have done and what exactly it is that they accomplished for the site. If you are using one of the previously mentioned websites or another site, many of them have ratings on each freelancer. Previous completed projects are shown, as well as feedback from other people who have used them to do a job.

This can provide great insight on the person's record, timeliness, and accuracy, as well as buyer satisfaction. It takes some time to build up positive feedback, so this is a good indicator of their track record as well. It is much like the feedback you see on eBay: it provides you with an inside look at how others have dealt with the person in the past on other jobs.

No freelancer you speak with should have any problems providing you with a record of their past work. They understand that this is how you will make a final decision on who you choose to complete the tasks you need to get done. If you feel any sense of doubt or hesitation, do not hire someone just because you may feel a little bit guilty.

Many times, freelancers get turned down for jobs, but they can always move on to another one. If you think the person is not capable of giving you the high quality of work you expect within a certain amount of time, politely let them know you have chosen someone else to finish the job and move on to the next person.

Getting a freelance job is much like auditioning for a part in a play. The person must show their skills and talents to you, and then you as the director has to make a final decision based on what you see. It also depends on the type of work you need done. For example, you cannot afford errors when it comes to getting some coding done for your website. An ebook or content provider may not need to have as stringent guidelines.

Ultimately, the choice is up to you, so review all work carefully. Ask for portfolios, writing samples, references, and even resumes, depending on the thoroughness of the job. You can usually tell who will do a good job for you, so follow your instincts and intuition.

Think of using someone in outsourcing just like hiring someone to work in your office. You want them to be honest, trustworthy, accurate, and efficient. Only you can make this final call, but by using the various resources and websites available for freelancers, you have a better chance at finding someone you really want to use time and time again.

Remember that you can always just use people for one small project and then move on to someone else if you're not happy with the results or the work.

In outsourcing, nothing is written in stone about the buyer. You are in control, since you set the budget, the requirements, and the needs you have in regard to what it will take to get the job done.

The Internet is full of extremely talented, gifted, and orga-nized people who have a real passion for what they do. You might choose one person for a job, and then move on to a different person for the same or similar job later down the line. Outsourcing is great because you do not have to be tied down to one person to do the jobs you need done. It's a wonderful way to network and find new talent as well. Use the outsourcing websites to make contacts and get together a team of virtual employees who can help you get things finished while freeing up your time to focus on other things.

As a business owner, you already have a definite goal in mind. Use your goals to project that same attitude onto the free-lancers you choose, so they fully understand what it is you need completed. Look for people with a positive and friendly attitude, and people who respond to your communications on a fairly quick basis.

Those who can keep to deadlines are those you will want to keep for a longer period of time. Make connections and ask those you hire to do jobs for referrals for other assignments. They may know someone else who can assist you with other goals such as graphic design or ebooks.

## What should be included in a project?

If you've finally made a decision on what you need and have chosen someone to complete the assignment or project, or if you're in the infant stages of listing your project, be sure you thoroughly state your needs. For example, if you need content written, list the topics the content will be about. Include the number of words you need as well as the number of articles written. Be sure to list the price that you are willing to pay for the articles, whether as a completed set, per word, or per article. This way, eligible candidates know ahead of time exactly what you are looking for, and how much you're willing to pay.

For coding jobs, show candidates an example of your site. Let them know in as much detail as possible the type of coding you will need and what needs to be done. For all listings, be as thorough as possible in regard to what your business is about. State the type of business you have, the attitude you're looking for, and the tone. What you say in your "help wanted" listing is crucial, since this will be what people look at in order to decide whether or not they want to assist you with the project.

Devise an outline of each project you need completed. Write it down clearly, and know exactly what you want to see accomplished, as well as your goals and timeframe for completion. Then, pass these requirements on to the person you choose to do the job.

This will help them get a very clear concise picture of what it is you're exactly looking for. If you try hard to make it as simple yet detailed as you can, the odds are in your favor that the person you pick to finish the project will do it to your liking and your specs. Remember, a project is only as good as the person who created it, so by giving very simple yet clear instructions, you'll see much better results.

If you need an ebook written, let people know exactly what you need in regard to the subject and the length of the book. If you need it written in chapters, specify that. If you need the person writing the ebook to state all references they use, be sure to list that as well. By being as specific as possible, you can assure that the project will be completed per your needs and that the person competing it will do the job to the best of his or her ability. This also saves time, since the candidate knows exactly what's needed in advance and this leaves little room for errors or time-consuming editing. When a job is done right the first time, it eliminates the back and forth of emailing, and saves you time from having to go over the submitted project and list all of the corrections needed.

All projects that are completed should include exactly what you've asked for, and in what format, so state this ahead of time. For example, if you need SEO content in Word format, the person needs to turn it in this way. If your ebook should be in PDF format this would apply as well, or a picture that you require to be in Adobe Photoshop format or JPG format. By being specific about the file format ahead of time, you are saving both yourself and the freelancer you've hired a lot of unnecessary headaches. As stated before, be as clear and detailed as to what you need as possible, so there is less room for error and for edits.

Thinking ahead of the curve will save you lots of time and money when it comes to outsourcing. By being open and honest, as well as upfront about what you need, you are helping to ensure you will get only the best people to complete your projects. Do not be afraid to turn work back over to the freelancer and have them fix any errors or problems. After all, this is your money and your business and anyone in freelancing already knows that it is their job to return high quality work to you. Make sure you are very clear about what you want and need in advance, and this will help you avoid problems later on.

Anything you pay money for as a business owner, whether it is a service offered by others such as web hosting, or an assignment you've given to someone to be outsourced, should be done to your utmost satisfaction. By using websites that hire or use highly qualified people, you are making sure you get the best of the best. After all, this is your time, your money, and your business.

All projects you receive should be completely finished and next to perfect before you pay for them. Don't just accept second best. Never pay for a service or project unless it is finished, correct, and thorough. You can be sure this will happen if you already have a picture in your mind about what you want the project to look like or consist of. Knowing this in advance gives everyone a better edge to be successful.

## Ways to get your project at a cheaper price

Since it is your money that you'll be spending out of pocket for various outsourced projects, you want to be sure you are getting the best deal and the best price possible. Negotiation is usually a good way to start. Set a limit in advance about the maximum amount of money you will be willing to spend and try your best not to go over it.

Often, freelancers are willing to negotiate prices, since this is the bulk of their income, and freelance work can be hard to come by. If you ask for a project and the person does not like the amount you want to pay, see if you can get them to add a few extra things to the project, such as an extra graphic or an additional article. Often people will take the price you offer upon agreement to do just a little bit of extra work. Bartering for services is another idea to help you get a good price on your outsourcing needs. For example, you can offer the person who wants to do the job a free service that you offer in exchange for the completed project. You can offer them web related referrals in exchange as well. Many times, you can trade services instead of paying out cash and this is an excellent money saver.

Negotiate your project price carefully, however. Many people will turn a job down in the long run if the pay rate is too low. Think carefully about how you want to negotiate, and make sure both of you are communicating clearly and often to avoid any misunderstanding.

Another way to get your project done at a cheaper price is to "buy in bulk." For example, let's say you need 15 articles written. Instead of paying for each individual article, you can offer to pay a flat fee for all 15 articles at once for a lesser price. Many people understand the concept of doing a list of projects for a flat fee, and this enables you to get more for your money. A lot of the freelance bidding websites will let you post projects on a multiple or bulk basis. You can get more accomplished at a much cheaper cost this way.

Advertise work you need done on free job boards. Sometimes you can find a local person who can help you for a low fee. Usually these people are easy to work with since they're close and they may do the work for a discount for you since you can simply pick it up or call them on the phone through a local call.

Negotiate prices with everyone you come in contact with unless they are willing to do the job you need completed at a lower price than you've budgeted yourself for. Many people opt to pay new freelancers that they've hired a lower fee for the first few assignments, but if they like the work they do, as they progress, they often increase the pay rate.

Brainstorm other ways you can get the things you need done without spending a pretty penny. Look for people who are able to do more than one job at a time for you and are experts in many different fields. This way, you may be able to get them to finish projects for you at a reduced cost.

They might be able to finish two or more projects at one time, for one flat fee or rate. Buying your jobs in bulk is a great way to save money. Think about the different ways you can get more work done for less bucks. It will be an invaluable tool for you to make more time for yourself and your business, thus making you more money in the long run.

With so many things happening today in business at the speed of light, you do not always have time to cover all of your bases. However if you neglect certain aspects of your job or your business, you could end up shooting yourself in the foot. This is where outsourcing comes in.

By choosing an outside person or source to assist you with your business needs, you are making a very smart move. Not only will you save loads of time, but also, you're getting things done without spending the excess overhead. This is invaluable for small businesses. Assigning projects to willing professionals at a set rate allows you to stay within your budget while still allowing you to get important aspects of your business up and running.

The Internet now provides so many wonderful resources for outsourcing that the possibilities are endless. By looking for websites that offer qualified people and a structured method of payment, you can maximize your time and look for people who will get things done for you in a timely and professional manner. In many cases you will find someone who you can count on permanently, who will accept projects from you on an individual basis as often as you need them.

Outsourcing can also offer you new ways of thinking about your business that you might not have thought of before. You may end up finding a good group of people who can assist you with new ideas, great graphics, website content, and other brainstorming concepts that can bring your business to a whole new level.

By enlisting the help of others through outsourcing, you are really broadening your horizons with a fresh outlook and a new method of getting things done. You may also find that you really like outsourcing your projects to others, and that it will help you to organize other aspects of your business, giving you more time for networking, meetings and focusing on expansion in other ways.

There is a wide, wide range of talent online today with so many skilled and experienced freelancers that you will be surprised by how much truly reliable and outstanding talent is out there. Choosing your group of people personally gives you the freedom to make choices on whom you want to work with you and your business.

It also opens up the doors to a new opportunity to accomplish goals in a much timelier fashion. Make a list of the things you need done, and then check out the number of helpful websites available today that offer a group of experienced freelancers who can handle any task. Outsourcing may seem like an overhead expense at first, but in essence it is really a solid investment in your business and its future.

At first, the term outsourcing might invoke feelings of uneasiness or uncertainty about the quality of work you will receive. Rest assured, by using certified websites like elance.com, rentacoder.com, and many others, you can find helpful people who are willing to assist you in any way you need. The work gets done on time, and its quality work with a guarantee before you make payment.

Both sides benefit, making it a win win situation for you and the other parties involved. Don't be afraid to enlist the help of others if you feel like you're becoming overwhelmed with the number of tasks you need completed. By outsourcing, you can be sure your tasks are completed on time and to your satisfaction, all while freeing up more time for you to focus on other things.

Even the most ardent business owners run into issues, deadlines, and overwhelming tasks they need to get done. Enlisting the help of a freelance worker through outsourcing is an excellent way to ensure you get the job done in the timeframe you have allotted, and you can also be sure it will be done to your satisfaction.

Have no fear; outsourcing online today is one of the most effective ways that small Internet businesses get things completed. Don't be afraid to explore and try out different small tasks through outsourcing, just to get a feel for how the process works. Eventually you will be surprised at how easy it is to use others to assist you with your tasks.

Thinking of outsourcing as an investment has proven to be a great way for businesses to get things accomplished that may have otherwise been on the backburner for months. With the help of others, you will find that the job you thought could or would never get done is getting finished in a matter of days.

You will be amazed at how helpful outsourcing others can be if you find the right people. Set goals, set standards, and know what you're looking for. Decide on how much you're willing to budget, and then put your project out there for others to see. You will be able to find reliable, accurate, and professional people who can help you get your business on track by providing services and finishing tasks you may have never had the time to finish yourself.

# CHAPTER 7

## LAUNCHING A WEBSITE FOR YOUR BUSINESS

Launching a website is a process. Many people seem to think you can simply create a website and upload it and it will magically start making money, but that's just not true. Even if you have a large email list at your disposal, sometimes that's not enough to make a website successful.

In this chapter, you're going to uncover the major steps it takes to launch a website successfully. These tips are geared specifically toward product launches, but they can certainly apply to any type of website launch including blogs. You will want to start your pre- launch campaign at least 2-4 weeks before launch. Any longer than that and the buzz will wane before launch, and any closer to launch and you won't have enough time for the buzz to spread. An important part of launching a website or product is planning, so be sure to plan your launch strategy out day by day before launch. This will help keep your organized and right on point.

## Pre-launch buzz

Perhaps the most important phase in a website launch is the building of buzz before the launch. If you release a website without first building buzz, the launch probably isn't going to go very well. You may have heard the common marketing idea that it takes at least three times of hearing a marketing message before the average person responds. The first time they hear it, they will often ignore it. The second time, they may be slightly interested, but they quickly forget. The third time they hear it, it finally begins to sink in, and they will remember it and act on it if they are interested.

Building pre-launch buzz takes advantage of this by inundating potential visitors with your message before the site launches. Not only does it help get the word out about the launch, but it gets people excited about the site before it even launches. There are many ways to create pre-launch buzz. We're going to look at a few of them in this report, but it's a good idea to think of some of your own, too. Originality is important.

## Videos

Videos are great for creating buzz, because they can be interesting, they can grab attention, and they're easy for people to share. If your video is interesting enough or helpful enough, people will start sharing it with their friends and family. This is called "going viral". Viral videos have the potential to reach thousands of people, sometimes millions, quickly and easily, with very little work. When you create a video, make sure it really speaks to your audience. You can't just make a sales video. It should provide real value to prospective visitors or buyers, and it should obviously be related directly to your niche or your product.

## Giveaways

Giveaways have a lot of power to generate buzz. People love free stuff, and they'll go to incredible lengths to potentially get it. If you can set up a special script, you can open a giveaway that gives people another entry into the giveaway for every person they refer. This helps spread the word quickly.

## Contests

In addition to standard giveaways, you can also hold contests to generate buzz. There are so many types of contests you could hold that could really get people excited. You should get creative when planning your contest and try to tie it into your niche. Let's say you're launching a weight loss product. You could hold a trivia contest and give away free copies of your product to the top 5 winners. You could ask people to send in "before" shots of themselves or create videos and submit them to YouTube about why they want a free copy of your product. Get creative with your contest and how it ties in with your product or website and it will be very rewarding!

## Live webinars

A webinar is a seminar that is held online. They are usually educational in nature, and they can be very powerful if you really make people believe the information you'll be giving will be valuable to them.

## Traffic

Creating marketing pieces for pre-launch buzz is important, but they can't do you any good if no one sees them. You need a lot of traffic to get the buzz going. Many types of traffic aren't suitable for the pre-launch phase, because they take too long to bring in. You need immediate, instantaneous traffic, because you need to ensure the traffic comes in when you need it – before launch. We're going to take a look at some of the different sources of traffic that work well for launches.

## Social marketing

Sites like Twitter and Facebook are great for creating buzz because they are in real-time. As soon as you post something, it is visible to everyone who is following you. Obviously, you will need a targeted list of followers for this to be effective. If you have 10,000 followers who aren't targeted, your response will likely be negligible. If you have 500 followers who are very well-targeted to your niche, your response could be phenomenal!

Don't forget to ask your followers to re-tweet or repost your messages. This will help you reach people who aren't following you.

## Email

If you have an email list, you will obviously want to use it for sending out your pre-launch messages. But what if you don't have a list of your own? You can make use of other people's lists! You can buy a message in a newsletter very cheaply, or you can buy a solo mailing that will be much more effective, but it will cost a lot more. I highly recommend solo mailings because you want your message to be the sole focus. If you buy a spot in a newsletter, your message could get lost in the shuffle. If you can afford it, I recommend buying solo emails from several of the most high-traffic newsletters in your niche.

## Joint ventures

If you have your own list, you can multiply its potential by offering to do joint ventures with other people who own lists in your niche. Let them know you're planning to launch a new website or product, and that you're looking to generate as much buzz as possible before the launch. Let them know the launch date, as well as the anticipated date for beginning the pre-launch phase. That way, they can schedule your mailing so it won't conflict with anything else they need to mail out around that time. Ask them to email out for you, and in exchange you will mail your list about something for them in the future. It's the perfect win-win situation if both parties have comparably sized email lists.

## Affiliates

What if you can't afford a solo mailing and you don't have your own email list? If you are launching a product, you can have affiliates do the mailing for you without paying them up front! You may need to have a special script made in order to track pre-launch traffic. Since you won't be able to have affiliates send traffic directly to an affiliate link before the site launches officially, you will have to set things up to track affiliate clicks before the product can even be bought. This will mean you will need to set up a cookie that won't expire before launch, or you will need another tracking method. You may want to offer pre-launch affiliates a special commission. If your normal commission if 50%, you might offer affiliates who promote during the pre-launch phase a 65% commission. This will be an incentive to get them to promote you before you're ready to take orders.

## Pay-per-click

Pay-per-click traffic is great for generating pre-launch buzz, but you have to use it wisely. Since you won't be taking payments immediately, you will need to use the traffic to build a list that you can announce to on launch day. Be prepared to spend quite a bit of money up front, and you may not make it back right away.

# CHAPTER 8
## JOINT VENTURE MASTERY

Joint ventures are a great way to promote your product without having to spend a lot of money up front on traffic. You can leverage your own resources to multiply your own promotional efforts, and you can benefit others by helping them with their own promotions. Profitable joint ventures are a win-win situation for both parties. Done correctly, a joint venture can be extremely beneficial for everyone involved.

In this chapter, you're going to discover what a joint venture really is, how to use them profitably, and how to find people who would love to be your joint venture partner.

Remember, a joint venture should be beneficial to both parties. Make sure you focus equal time on making your joint venture partners happy, and they will reward you with more traffic than you could ever get on your own!

### What is a joint venture?

A joint venture is a mutually beneficial relationship in which one party promotes the product of another party, and in return the party whose product is promoted agrees to similarly reciprocate. In some ways, being a JV partner is like being an affiliate. You're promoting someone else's product in exchange for compensation, but instead of being paid in cash, you are paid by having your own product promoted in return.

Usually, joint ventures involve email lists. This isn't always true, but in the majority of cases it is. In the next section, we're going to take a look at some of the different types of joint ventures.

All JVs should be equally beneficial to both parties. If one party benefits far more than the other party, it can't be mutually beneficial, and you probably won't be able to JV with that person again in the future. Build relationships, not money!

## Types of joint ventures

There are many different ways to develop mutually beneficial joint ventures. We're going to look at a few of the ways you can build the most effective joint ventures.

## Email joint ventures

The most common type of joint venture is when two parties who have email lists of similar sizes agree to email their own lists for each other. Let's say you have an email list of about 5,000 people and you meet someone who has a list of around 7,000 people.

Chances are good that a good portion of your list will not be on their list and vice versa. That means each of you could reach many more people by cooperating and sending emails out for each other. Email joint ventures work well as long as lists are within about 50% of each other.

If you have a list of 10,000 people, you could JV with someone with 15,000 people or someone with 12,500 people, but not 20,000 people or 5,000 people. If one party has more than 50% more subscribers, both parties may not feel satisfied. You can JV with anyone who will agree to JV with you, but it's a good idea to make sure all of your JVs are as mutually beneficial as possible to keep the relationship preserved for the future.

## Traffic exchanges

If you don't have an email list, but you do have a website or blog with significant traffic, you can do a traffic exchange with someone else in your niche with similar traffic.

Generally, the traffic you send to your JV partner won't be exactly on par with what they send you. Even if both websites have the same amount of traffic, visitors aren't likely to respond evenly to different offers. As long as both parties understand going into the business relationship that there is no way to guarantee equal response, traffic exchanges can definitely be beneficial. Just do your best to make sure you reciprocate as evenly as possible and both parties should be relatively satisfied.

## Cross promotions

When you release a product, you can form a partnership with someone who has a product that complements your product well. Let's say your product is a book about losing weight with a low- calorie diet. You could do a cross promotion with someone who offers a calorie counter software program. They could promote your program as the best weight loss program to work with their software, and you could promote their software as the best software to use to keep track of calories with people who are using your weight loss system.

Cross promotions are another type of mutually beneficial relationship that can work really well. Again, both parties need to understand that the response they receive or the money they make may not be perfectly aligned with the other party's outcome. There is no way to ensure a perfectly even reciprocation, but that doesn't mean both parties can't be happy.

## Finding JV partners

Perhaps the hardest part of joint venturing is finding people to form JV partnerships with. It can be very difficult to find JV partners, especially if you don't already have a big name in your niche. When you contact potential JV partners, you need to make sure to let them know what's in it for them. Don't talk extensively about yourself. Don't talk extensively about your product. Talk about what you can do for them. You need to make sure you let them know why they should JV with you. While it is important to tell them a bit about yourself and your product, you should focus on why it would be beneficial for them. Now, let's take a look at a few ways to find potential JV partners. There are many other ways, but we're just going to take a look at some of the easiest and most popular ways to find potential JV partners.

## Contacting potential JV partners

One of the easiest ways to find JV partners is to locate people in your niche that have large email lists or high-traffic websites or blogs and contact them. Many websites have contact forms or pages you can use. You may be able to find email addresses or telephone numbers. If not, you can check WHOIS.net. You may be able to get contact information that way.

## Forums

Webmaster forums and JV forums are great for finding potential JV partners. There are forums dedicated specifically to JVs, and general webmaster forums can also be helpful.

Try these:

- warriorforum.com

- digitalpoint.com

- jvnotifypro.com

## JV brokers

Try these:

- jointventurebroker.net

- williecrawford.com

- Master Joint Ventures

## Tracking results

In order to ensure that your joint ventures are as profitable as possible, you need a way to track the results you get from each partner. You want to ensure that your partners are living up to their part of the bargain, and you want to make sure you know how well they performed in case you JV with them at a later date. Instead of having JV partners send traffic directly to your domain, you should have them send traffic through a special link so you can track results. This could be somewhat like an affiliate link. If you have software that can track it, this can work well.

If you don't have special software that can track results, you can have traffic sent through a simple script. You can easily get a PHP script that will let you redirect traffic through a special link and will track the traffic that goes through each link. Just find a link cloaking script that tracks traffic and you'll be able to easily measure the results you get from each partner. You may also be able to track sales by setting up a system like Google's Website Optimizer.

# Chapter 9
## EBOOK MARKETING

An ebook is one way to get an individual's ideas online either for free or for a reasonable price tag. Basically the term ebook refers to the electronic form of publication of any information. The information can be on a vast and almost infinite variety of topics and the information can also be sources from other online postings.

### Ebook basics

Most ebooks use the PDF format but there are also other formats that can be used without many problems while producing the same results. The individual would have to ensure the electronic format used is compatible otherwise the information would not be able to be accessed easily therefore defeating the purpose of the posting.

### The basics

The process of successfully churning out an ebook is not very difficult and with a little bit of knowledge and research one should be able to come up with a presentable piece worth posting. For the more experienced and serious ebook authors this is a very lucrative revenue-earning platform. The following are some tips on how to get started:

Ensure one has a word processor that saves information in PDF formats. Google Docs, which is free, Microsoft Word, which is not available for free, and Open Office, which is also free, can get the job done adequately.

The next step, which for most can be quite challenging is to be able to come up with material that is worth sharing or selling. This material has to be original in its content in order to be able to draw the attention of the target audience and to also create a sense of expertise and trustworthiness for the author. Copied works are usually not favorably look upon.

Print or save the written material in PDF. Deciding on a set number of words would also be wise as material that is too lengthy can be off putting for some.

## Decide how your ebook will be used

There are several different ways to use an ebook compilation online today. Some of these are specifically designed as market-able revenue earning product while other are the contributions of individuals who just want to share information with others and yet others who write ebooks as a way to indulge in a writing passion that they have.

## The point

Whatever the reasons may be the ebooks that are produced will usually be done in a fashion that best suits its purpose for creation.

Those who choose to create ebooks for the purpose of establishing steady revenue earning platforms will definitely be more serious and conscientious about its content and design as compared to those who simply do so for the sheer pleasure of being able to share their views and knowledge.

The one that chooses to do so as an earning tool will focus more on getting the information that is the most relevant, recent and fact based. Being a tangible asset the ebooks are something that can be tapped for its profit churning capabilities at any given place and time.

The sale of such ebooks can be done individually whereby the author has to actively promote his or her ebooks to parties interested in purchasing them or the other option would be to sign on with an already established entity that specializes in churning out ebooks to others for a fee.

Ebooks can also be designed to create an individual's presence within a specified platform. The individual would then be perceived as an authority on the subject matter being produced through the ebook, thus creating a need for the said individual to be needed for their contributions.

Creating ebooks is considered a big business entity for today's information hungry world. Almost anyone can create an ebook when armed with the adequate amount of corresponding information.

## Decide on formats relative to how your ebook will be used

Deciding on the format most suitable for the types of various possible uses of the ebook is most important to ensuring its effectiveness. It is considered by those who are better informed

COMBAT BOOTS TO MARKETING PRO

as an essential point to consider when it comes to electronic publishing styles.

## Formatting

The format eventually chosen after the relevant considerations have been made will determine the nature of the digital package in which it is distributed. There are many new formats that are available, and many more new ones being developed. Currently there are tools available to facilitate the repackaging of existing formats into other acceptable or customs designed formats for alternative use.

This is of course very useful when the decision is made to commit to one style early on in the designing phase of the ebook exercise.

Considering the compatibility of the target audience in accessing and browsing through the content of the ebook is important. If the target audience intended is unable to access the information posted on the ebook through the chosen format, then the ebook would not be worth anything to them besides of course the more obvious element of frustration they would experience when trying to access the said information.

Creating ways to ease the installation and use for the intended target audience is also another important point to consider. Here too if the installation process is lengthy and tedious the definite existence of the user-unfriendly aspect of the design would be off putting and frustrating.

Therefore it is necessary to look into the installation requirements so that one that is easy can be tailored to fit the accessibility of the ebook.

The supporting tools that maybe required in order for the special features to be viewed without any interruptions must also be well chosen. There is nothing more annoying for the user than to have these interruptions marring the general experience of the ebook browsing.

## Choose a relevant topic

As ebooks are predominantly designed for a specific target audience there should ideally be some thought put into the topic matter to be featured in it.

The content provided in the ebook should ideally reflect the information, solutions, problem encounters and other related material that would be useful to the reader focused that the particular subject.

Therefore choosing topic to write about should be done with some thought and care to ensure the choice made is interesting, attention grabbing and competitive in the ebook arena of current times.

## Suggestions

The following are some suggestions of how to choose relevant topics:

Determining and understanding the reasons for writing the ebook should be clearly established even before the exercise to write begins. Questions such as is it being written for monetary gain, promotional reasons, expansion of knowledge, creating an online presence or any of the other motivating reasons should be addressed.

Conducting a thorough market research exercise to determine what is currently causing a "buzz" and the online keywords that are popularly used is also another way to determine a suitable choice topic to write on.

Considering a topic that has a personal connection to the individual is also something that can be explored as such material is often well received as others are able to relate to such personal style content.

"How to" ebooks are another popular option to choose to write on. However if one decides to do this kind of ebook the information contained in the book should be both of sound and substantiated material. A lot of research and thought needs to be put into this style of content.

Having a brainstorming session with colleagues, friends, family and basically anyone who is willing to listen or already connected to the ebook scene, to come up with topics is also a viable way to get ideas.

## Put your ebook together

There are several software's available in the market today to assist in the exercise of ebook compiling. Some may seem complicated while others may seem too technical, so the following points are designed to create an easy step by step guide for putting together a simple ebook presentation.

## Put it together

Following the ebook compiler options the individual would have to assign a suitable title for the intended ebook listing and then enter the content about the page while setting the ebook's window parameters.

Using the ebook compiler files the next step would be to select the ebook folder and set up the order of the files and assign a startup page.

For security reasons the individual would be expected to set up the user password with a combination of serial numbers for the intended ebook posting.

The toolbar usage would require the ebook compiler toolbar icon to be keyed in. the individual would have to select the buttons, assign the captions for the chosen buttons and icons for the toolbar corresponding actions.

The ebook compiler bookmarks are where the individual would insert bookmarks or links that would be displayed at the navigational page of the ebook design content.

Generating the branding capabilities through the e-brander with the selection parameters can be done in the ebook compiler branding phase.

The compilation stage of the process requires the individual to create and save the ebook.

Using other time saving tips when compiling the ebook is also encouraged. Another ebook compiler tip that is rather useful in the pop-up tool tips points.

This tool is accessed whenever the individual places the cursor over any area that requires some sort of action. The tool tip information will then appear informing the viewer of the next course of action that needs to be taken to proceed smoothly.

This is better than having to revert to the manual and wasting a substantial amount to precious time and energy.

## Arrange the ads in your ebook

Though not widely accepted at the moment arranging ads for ebooks is fast gaining some level of popularity. The revenue earner is nowhere near phenomenal, yet it would be something interesting and beneficial to consider.

## Ads

The popular question that is currently hotly debated is whether or not ebooks should feature ads and if so, how much should the authors receive in terms of revenue percentages.

Some ebook designers are now including platforms for advertising applications to facilitate revenue earning possibilities. Though it is still considered unfamiliar territory there are visible concerted efforts made to tap into this possibility for the future.

Attracting advertisers to the ebooks is an ongoing exercise but unlike other media there is some level of ambiguity when it comes to the accurate projection of sales derived from ebooks.

Some advertising can be comfortably applied to the particular device or brand author with a proven track record for sales to the digital versions made.

Then there is the possibility of garnering smaller advertising revenue projections which might be available to a target-based audience for specific content. However meaningful projections of sales percentages which are to be based on corresponding advertising costs may prove to be rather difficult. There are also those that are quite against the idea of including ads in the ebook style of publications as it is currently perceived to be somewhat annoying and cumbersome.

Those who choose not to be interrupted by such ads basically download applications that stop such interruptions adequately thus defeating the overall intentions of advertising in the first place.

There is also the issue of interactive availability and color screen help when it comes to viewing the ad on an ebook. To date both these issues though being addressed by the relevant experts it has reached a level where the ebook user gets optimum quality visual effects.

## Decide what extras to include in your ebook

Designing an ebook is no longer just that. There should be other beneficial element added to the general makeup of the ebook to make it more competitive. Exploring the various possibilities would be advantageous and definitely create the platform for more interest and revenue earnings.

## The extras

The first and important step to take would be to ensure the material posted is done in a PDF format although HTML versions are also acceptable though not as accommodating. Apart from the revenue earning potential there is also the fact that ebooks present opportunities that ordinary printed information lacks.

Without restrictions in place such as using incompatible formats, the viewer should be able to access many platforms from the actual article posted.

From the viewers point of view, finding and accessing information should be made easy and quick therefore making the text "clickable" would be advantageous.

Being able to click on a particular chapter, title or any segment and then having it immediately pop up is something that would be time and energy saving thus be looked upon favorably.

Providing further extras such as facilitating a link on the ebook that opens a web page or even starts an email is also a good idea. With this facility the viewer can easily make other references from different sources and also access web links.

The email pop up can be used to get immediate feedback from the viewer which would help the host to address any shortcomings.

Making recommendations on other products, services or businesses can also be done in the ebook. When the viewer clicks through to the site where the new information is being posted the affiliate program can then bring in extra revenue to the host.

## Market your ebook depending on its use

Having a great ebook but marketing it without any real direction will bring about less than desirable results. Knowing the ebook contents and matching it with the target audience that will find the content suitable for their needs is an important factor to look into if the desired success rate is to be achieved.

## Marketing

Creating a market that is well served with the particular ebook is always a good idea and putting the relevant tools into practice to ensure this end will allow the ebook to be sold according to its particular niche market. Once this is established more viewers will be interested in making a firm purchase. Understanding that the ebook creator may not always be an authority on the current needs of the viewing public is a humble place to start.

Doing some research or arming yourself with supporting information before the niche market is approached for the purpose of getting the ebook well received should be done at the very onset of deciding the marketing strategy.

Conducting surveys, keeping abreast with current comments on blogs, reading material from popular forums or any other information that can shed light on the perceptions toward the content of the ebook in the market will assist the ebook owner to make better judgments on who would be best served by viewing the said ebook.

This would then enable the owner to focus the attention on this group to promote the book to. Understanding the customer is basically looking for real solutions when they source for ebook will also assist in being able to promote the ebook according to its use. The target audience should be able to connect with the material in the ebook if it is to achieve any level of success.

## Launching your product

The following are some tips which should ensure a successful launch strategy:

## Putting it together

Offering a pre-launch discount or even freebies to all those on the individual's emailing list would be a good way to start the attention-grabbing campaign for the launch of the ebook. This action will also contribute to the loyalty status of those on the email list.

Making the launch more attractive by adding features that include bonus earning potential for committed buyers is also encouraged. Most people will be more inclined to make a commitment if there is something else to be gained besides the intended product itself.

Hiring outside help with the proper tools and knowledge on how to make a successful launch is something that should be considered especially if previous launches did not live up to expectations. Sometimes this is not only cost effective but also a less stressful option.

Making a good first impression is sometimes the only way to ensure a successful launch. It is therefore in the best interest of the ebook design to have an attention-grabbing cover design. It may even be necessary to hire a professional who would have a better idea on what is sellable.

Keeping track of every aspect of a launch is also necessary and using good supportive tools that can ensure this would be an advantage. If the monitoring system chosen is adequate there is will less stress for the individual as everything would be visible and accessible at a moment's notice. If there are any problems detected within the launching process it can be addressed immediately and effectively.

## Wrapping Up

There are a lot of things one can do to ensure the ebooks are well received. Some may take a little more time and effort than others but ultimately, they all are designed to garner as much attention and revenue to the launch of the ebook.

# Chapter 10
## Knocking Out Your Competition (USP Formula)

Have you been struggling to compete and stand out in your market? Are you fighting your way through a never-ending crowd of merchants, feeling as though you'll never be able to generate the exposure that your business needs in order to survive?

If so, chances are that the reason why you haven't been able to generate the kind of business you'd been hoping for is because you're not giving people a reason to buy from you!

In today's market, it's easy to slip into the huddle of new businesses that are cropping up within your market. In fact it's dangerously easy to end up being nothing more than a "me, too!" business owner where your voice is drowned out by the sound of every other similar business in your industry.

And in today's market, the ONLY way that you'll ever be able to build a business that stands on its own and is successful over the long-haul is by discarding the safety of the "me, too!' space and separating from the crowd.

And my friend, the only way to do this is with a USP.

A what?

USP stands for Unique Selling Proposition (or Position), and it can literally make or break your business because it tells your target audience exactly why you are different, what you bring to the table and why they should choose you, over the competition.

Without a USP, your product slinks into the shadows, barely able to compete in the marketplace.

It doesn't stand out nor does it leave an everlasting impression in the minds of your prospects. In fact, without a USP it's virtually impossible to create a unique brand that will be instantly associated to value because you haven't defined what makes your business special. People will never recognize you as being any different from your competition.

The great news is that your business, or product already has a USP. It's simply your job to define what that is and implement it into your marketing message so that your target audience knows exactly what you are offering, how they will benefit and most importantly, why they should go to your company or business, rather than the competition.

So, where do you begin? How can you figure out what your USP is and how to deliver your message to your audience of potential customers?

It all begins by evaluating your business, your products, and your offers.

- How can what you offer improve someone's life?

- How can it help your customer in some way?

- Why do they need it?

- Why should they purchase from you rather than the competition?

- What are you offering that other people aren't?

Evaluating your product – your business and your offers objectively, from a third person perspective is incredibly important. It's the only real way to determine your strengths and your weaknesses so that you can improve your business, reach out to your global audience, and give them a genuine reason to come to you. And when you do this, you will never struggle in the market again because your USP will be the leading force that drives in non-stop business for many years to come.

## Knowing your customer base

Before you can create your USP for your business, you need to know your target audience – your customer base. What is most important to them? How can you truly connect to your target audience? What is their greatest challenge and how can you help them overcome it?

The more you know your audience, the easier it will be to develop a USP that hits home with them – that provokes a positive response and really shows your customer base that you know what they need.

When creating your USP, think from your customers perspective so that rather than identifying what YOU may feel is most important about your product, you turn it around - and focus on what THEY want to know and feel is most important to them.

Dan Kennedy's method for identifying a USP is in answering the question, "Why should I choose to do business with you versus your competitor?"

The very reason why you created a product in the first place could hold the key to defining your USP. Think about how your product is different than others on the marketplace, how does it add more value? How does it address a question, concern, or simplify a process, such as reducing a learning curve, saving your customers time or money.

Your product USP is the driving force behind defining value and creating a recognizable brand in your market. There are businesses who have so carefully highlighted their USP that they are able to charge DOUBLE what their competitors charge, and still sell out every single time simply because their USP adds perceived value to their products or services!

One of the most well-known examples of an effective USP is Domino's Pizza. The business, struggling and close to filing Chapter 11, needed a quick turnaround. Hence, the USP, "Fresh, hot pizza delivered in 30 minutes or less or it's free" was coined.

Then there's Burger King who, competing against the McDonalds franchise giant had to stand out from the 'pre-made fast food service, and successfully did so by coining the USP, "Have it your way" where customers are able to customize their meals based on their preferences. They put customers in control, and the USP was successful at helping them stand out.

Other competitors in the pizza delivery business jumped on board, integrating powerful USP's into their marketing campaigns, including Papa John's restaurant whose USP promises "better ingredients, better pizza".

All of these businesses had existing competition yet became successful national franchises that are instantly recognized in their industry. They did this with the help of a powerful USP that made a clear promise and working to align your brand with delivering on that promise.

Your USP will differentiate you from your competition; more than any other aspect of a marketing campaign ever will, but you need to make sure your USP is not only memorable, but believable.

Using Federal Express as an example, their USP is "when it absolutely, positively has to be there overnight", emphasizing their guarantee of prompt delivery service. "Absolutely, positively" reinforces that promise, adding extra punch to their USP while ensuring they can follow through.

You want your USP to clearly define your brand, separate you from the competition and be believable.

In today's marketplace, your business will struggle to stand out from the crowd without a USP to give that extra boost it needs, so that it instantly offers an added incentive for prospects who are making the decision between purchasing your product or your competitors.

Take your time when developing your USP. Think of ways that you can add unique flare to your product, how you can use your USP to demonstrate value, to illustrate performance, and to showcase the distinctive benefits of your product.

Your USP should be described in a couple of sentences. You want to keep it short and to the point so that it lends "stickiness" to your campaigns and becomes quickly (and permanently) associated to your brand.

Once you have defined your USP, you want to include it in every single marketing campaign. From newsletters, ezine advertisements, social media marketing, forum marketing, PPC advertisements, to your website itself.

## Creating a successful USP

USP's are far more than just catchy taglines associated to your company, product, or brand. They are reinforcement tools that help you establish credibility in your market while shaping the foundation of your business.

When it comes to creating a USP for your information product, think of the different ways that you can stand out from the competition, including:

Enhanced Training Tools, Additional Support Options, Extended Guarantee, Price Discounts, Better Service, Faster delivery/ turnaround time/completion, Additional Bonuses & Special Offers

All of these are common components of what forms a strong USP. Your objective is to evaluate your product and come up with a powerful unique selling proposition that you can integrate into your marketing campaigns.

The easiest way to come up with a powerful USP is to think about how you would describe your product if asked by a complete stranger that you met at a seminar. You are given ten minutes to describe your product in enough detail to sell a copy right on the spot.

What would you feel is most important to say about your business or offer within a 10-minute span of time?

This exercise will help get your creative juices flowing, while helping to verbalize the benefits of your product. Call a friend or family member if you have to and let them ask you questions about your product.

Not only will this help you to evaluate your product objectively, but you can often gain better insight as to what questions and concerns potential customers may have based on the questions you are asked.

If you have an existing channel of communication with your customer base, either through social media sites, community forums or perhaps even through a newsletter, ask for their feedback.

Offer a handful of customers a free copy of your product and let THEM evaluate it, providing important feedback based on what they felt were the most positive aspects of your product, as well as what could possibly use a bit of improvement.

Many times, your customers are the best sources for developing your USP because they know your product better than even you do. After all, you created it for them and you can gain a lot of incredibly valuable information just by letting them try it out and sharing their thoughts and ideas as to what the most powerful benefit of your product is.

Evaluating feedback from your customer base will also help you to develop a USP that carries a message that matches your market.

For example, if you develop an information product USP that defines your product as "Advanced Training for Beginners", you'll struggle to transfer positive branding if the majority of your market have virtually no experience and are looking for a product that teaches them the fundamentals of web design before considering advanced techniques. In other words, your USP message doesn't match your market.

So, survey your market, pay attention to feedback, and take a hands- on approach to closely monitoring the questions, concerns, and problems that your market is facing. Then, develop a USP that speaks directly to the core of what they are most interested in.

When you have evaluated your product, its competition and have decided on a USP for your product, you need to lead your USP by example.

This means that you might have to make changes to the way you do business, or how you present your product on your sales page, within marketing campaigns and in branding your product.

If your USP is "10 Minute Training for $10k per month", you want to make sure that your product is designed to provide quick access to bite size information that your customer base can instantly apply to their online business.

Make sure your product and USP match up, in every way. If you offer extended support in your USP, or you define your brand by being 'unique or exclusive', you need to make sure that your product offers a new perspective, a unique approach, or a different way of doing something.

## Price-based USP

If your product fails to carry a USP, the only way people will differentiate your product from a competitors' is on price alone.

Think about this in regard to your own buying decisions. If you were to visit your local computer shop with the intention of purchasing an external hard drive, knowing little about brands or features, and were presented with two similar products to choose from, which would you buy?

In the absence of any other differentiating factor, the lowest price becomes the deciding factor.

You never want to compete on a price based USP, because it leaves you little control over your markets decision whether to purchase from you or a competitor.

Instead, you need to develop a Unique Selling Proposition that uniquely separates you from other products in the marketplace and do so in such a way that it would be difficult for a competitor to replicate that.

Also keep in mind that your USP not only helps you stand apart but becomes part of your brand, so even if a competitor replicates your USP, if you've done your job at associating that unique selling proposition to your product, they'll struggle to compete.

## Integrating your USP

When you've decided on a USP for your product, you need to begin weaving into your marketing message.

This includes:

- Business Cards

- Your Sales Pages

- Squeeze Pages

- Print Advertising

- Social Media Advertising

Wherever you advertise or promote your business, your USP needs to become a permanent part of that marketing message.

You want your customers to identify you by your USP, and to solidify your place in the market by leveraging your USP to build instant recognition.

Your USP is more than just a tagline; it represents your brand and your commitment to fulfilling on your promise. You want your USP to communicate a positive benefit, to leave an everlasting impression with your target audience, and to nurture positive association to every other product you create.

One thing to keep in mind is that your USP can and sometimes, should, change if your market does. Of the examples from earlier, Domino's Pizza and Federal Express no longer use the original USP that was designed to give their businesses that extra push in the market.

Eventually their competitors started incorporating similar USP's into their own marketing campaigns and before too long, their USP's became ineffective.

After all, a USP is designed to help your business or product stand out in the marketplace, but if everyone else is using a similar USP, it can actually hinder your chances at building a recognized and unique brand. So they changed it, and you just might have to as well.

Your USP can help turbo charge your marketing efforts, but always be open to changing your USP as the market demand shifts, or as new competition enters the arena.

# CHAPTER 11
## BUSINESS BY COMMISSION - BOOSTING AFFILIATE SALES

You've joined the affiliate marketing industry, and you're excited about the opportunity to finally carve out a successful business online.

Perhaps you've already started making money in affiliate marketing, or you're a complete beginner - either way, it makes no difference because this chapter will show you exactly how you can maximize your income in this ever-growing arena.

Affiliate marketing is considered one of the easiest start-up businesses online, because rather than having to produce your own product you can start making money instantly - just by promoting other people's releases. However, in affiliate marketing, there's one key difference between struggling affiliates and super affiliates. That difference is the effort that they put into building profitable campaigns!

Super affiliates go the extra mile to provide exceptional value. They want their customers to be satisfied because after all, they are potentially lifetime customers.

Keep in mind that just because you are referring a customer to another merchant, rather than through your own product, they are still associating their purchase to you. You become the middleman, and once you've established trust within your audience, you'll be able to outsell any other affiliate marketer.

This chapter will give you the information you need to maximize sales quickly and easily. Whether you're brand new to affiliate marketing, or you've got some experience under your belt, these strategies will increase your overall profits.

## Enhancing value = Increased profit

When potential customers consider purchasing products, one of the first things that they ask themselves is, "what is the value of this product?" For many, the answer lies in how the product directly improves their lives or provides support or answers to their questions.

For others, especially seasoned buyers, they are constantly on the lookout for something else - Added Value.

Experienced buyers understand the dynamics of affiliate marketing, even if they are not involved in the industry themselves. They know that you are referring them to products because you earn a commission for doing so, and in return, they expect to be rewarded for purchasing from you, rather than another affiliate.

This is when bonus products that enhance value become so incredibly important. Bonus items can directly maximize your chances of making the sale, while building authority in your market as an affiliate that can be trusted.

You see, when you create bonus products that enhance the overall value of a product, you are giving your customers something more at absolutely no cost. You leave them very little reason not to purchase, while standing out from the crowd of affiliates who offer nothing more in return.

As to the types of bonus products you can offer, consider how they tie into the core product. You want your bonuses to add value, to serve as auxiliary components to the main product.

For example, if you were promoting a guide to blogging, you could offer a package of "ready-made" blog templates, blog content, or perhaps other tools and resources.

Just the same, your bonus could extend the training cycle, covering information not included in the main product.

For example, if you were selling a guide to work at home jobs, you could offer a bonus product that offered information on setting up a home office or creating a winning resume. Your bonus could also offer similar material, but in another format.

Since people prefer to learn in many different ways, you could offer a variety of material types, such as reports/ebooks, video training, webinars, transcripts, or audio lessons based around the core product's topic.

Plan out your bonuses carefully, making sure that they represent clear and distinct value. You should always assign a value price to all of your bonus items. Getting Started Online, "How To" Modules, Website Basics, Social Networking and more.

## Transforming content into cash

One of the easiest ways to siphon in customers and squeeze out more money from your affiliate campaigns is to become the leading "content authority" in your market.

This means that you have to over-deliver. You become second in command to the product developer, the original merchant, and position yourself, as an "authority affiliate" who people know will provide more value than anyone else will.

It's the winning formula to maximizing profit quickly, while actually having to do very little in exchange

One way of bundling in tons of extra value is to build your bonus around PLR (private label content). By doing this, you instantly eliminate two important factors:

1. You don't have to pay a fortune to outsource content to freelancers.

2. You don't have to spend any time creating content yourself.

Private label content also comes in many different forms, so you'll have greater access to tons of content that your customers want, such as:

## Complete tutorial guides

People love full sized collections of tutorials and guides, and you can easily compile your own by bundling together a variety of PLR based reports, guides, and ebooks.

## Done for you tools

If you can eliminate the learning curve and workload for your customers, you can easily make more money with every affiliate campaign.

Create a 'done for you' package around the product you are promoting and include as many different tools and resources as possible, each one designed to save customers time.

## Extended training

Even the greatest product on the market leaves room for improvement, and by compiling extra training tools out of private label content, you can extend the level of training to give customers a well-rounded system, designed to maximize their results.

One thing to be careful of is to only buy private label rights from authorized resellers and from quality developers. You can download as much private label content as you'll ever need at master-resale- rights.com including 500 full-length videos that you can repackage into 'auxiliary training tools' for your bonus!

## Building your business from other people's work

So, you are about to make money promoting a product from another merchant. Why not leverage the value of every customer by thinking beyond the front-end commission?

You can maximize your income instantly by taking things a step further and focusing on building YOUR business while promoting other people's products. You do this by building a targeted mailing list of your own!

You probably already know the importance of having a mailing list in any business online. It will give you instant access to a built-in customer base, help you solidify your place in the market and build a recognized brand. But did you know that even as an affiliate marketer, you can start building your own list without a product of your own?

You now understand the importance of creating bonus products as part of your affiliate marketing campaign, but here's where things get interesting. Rather than just offer a bonus as part of their purchase, you can offer additional FREE bonuses in exchange for their subscription to your list.

Sounds simple? That's because it is. You build a squeeze page around every product and topic you plan to promote, and on the squeeze page you highlight the key benefits of joining your list, including the free bonus items that will become available instantly after each visitor subscribes to your list.

Just make sure that your bonus ties in directly with the product you are promoting, so that you can build an individual mailing list for every market. This will make it easier to segment later on, so you can effectively target your core customers.

Your bonus offers can be anything imaginable, provided it adds direct value with the main product, including:

- Audio/Video Guides

- Ebooks & Reports

- Software & Graphics

- PLR Products (offer resell rights to your customers and give THEM a bonus they can offer their customers as well!)

- Courses

- Templates & Web Design elements

One critical part of the process is to "circulate" your bonus items. You don't want to offer the same item on your squeeze page for more than a few months before switching it up to offer something else.

That way, you don't have to worry about losing potential subscribers simply because they've seen the same bonus on another squeeze page.

Use private label as the foundation for all of your bonus products, and you'll be able to create new offers quickly and easily, every few months. Keeping your offers fresh!

## Final tips

Packing value into your affiliate campaigns is easy, even if you've never done it before. It will help you stand out in the marketplace, and will maximize your affiliate income instantly, just by giving more to your customers than they will find anywhere else.

When you position yourself as a super affiliate who has genuine interest in offering your customers extended value, you will never struggle to motivate customers to purchase through you. They would be silly not to!

Part of your affiliate plan of action should include creating your own creative media and material, so that you aren't using the same banners and graphics as everyone else. Plus, by creating your own banners and material you can customize it around your website theme, color scheme and preferences.

Get super high quality sales page graphics from iSalesGraphics.com

You don't need any design experience or technical "know-how" to get started. You can simply create instant graphics using this powerful website. All that's left is for you to take action and apply these strategies to your affiliate campaigns.

Focus on building a full inventory of bonus items that you can implement into existing campaigns and new ones that highlight clear value and motivate your customer base into taking action.

If YOU take action, they will too!

# Chapter 12
## PRIVATE LABEL CONTENT CASH

Does this sound anything like you? You are surprised to discover that you have a massive collection of un-used private label content stored haphazardly throughout your computer's hard drive.

When you purchased it, you were sure you'd earn your investment back quickly, because the PLR was advertised in such a way that it seemed like a great idea to use on your websites, in products and for creating content for your online marketing campaigns.

After all, private label content not only saves time, but because you don't need to hire-out someone to create custom content, you get to save a lot of money!

Then somewhere along the way, you simply forgot all about it, or you just haven't managed to monetize all of that private label content that you purchased.

Maybe you don't have a large collection of private label content now, but you've been seriously considering purchasing some of the newer releases available online.

If you are new to private-label buying, or if you've already got more private label content than you know what to do with, this chapter will show you how to monetize private label content instantly, so that you're able to make more money from every PLR package you own or buy!

So without further delay, let me show you exactly how to get started!

## The real value of PLR

I'm sure that I don't have to tell you that private label content is only as valuable as its quality. There are hundreds of PLR distributors online, some of which write their own content while others outsource cheap article content and package it up together in order to sell it with PLR rights.

When it comes to buying PLR, you truly get what you pay for. If you find yourself being attracted to the advertisements offering "thousands of PLR articles with unrestricted rights for $5.00", you'll want to reconsider your purchase.

Private label content should be written as if it were not intended to be PLR at all. In other words, if YOU wouldn't want to read it, and if you don't find the information valuable, helpful, or comprehensive, your customers won't either.

Apart from the quality of the content and material itself, you also want to consider the different licenses that are attached to PLR releases.

For the most part, you will want to avoid "unrestricted rights" because it entitles all buyers to distribute the content in virtually any way they wish, including re-selling the content cheaper, or giving it away. This kind of license may provide extended freedom, but it will also be saturated throughout your niche. This sort of content will be de-valued in a matter of days, due to its saturation throughout your niche.

To protect your investment, consider purchasing PLR that comes with either limited options and licenses (sold to fewer people with clear restrictions in place) or extended PLR, where PLR rights are given only to the buyers (not passed onto their customers and so on).

That way, you can avoid buying PLR that will be passed on to thousands of people, making it easier to sell to your customers with personal, non-transferable rights - just like any other high-quality product you release.

Many different private label developers online offer high quality content with limited rights.

You can explore one of the leading PLR communities at EnterpriseMembers.com where you can create a free account and gain access to brand new, all-inclusive private label packages. You can also explore premium PLR releases at Master-Resale- Rights.com

## How to monetize PLR – Today!

When it comes to making money with private label rights, there are many different options available to you.

You could:

- Rebrand the content as your own and sell with personal rights.

- Use the content to build quality authority-type websites and blogs.

- Power up auto responder systems or create a newsletter for your niche.

- Offer smaller segments of content as free downloadable reports.

- Create incentive offers for squeeze and landing pages.

You can also resell PLR content 'as is', or you could:

- Hire an affordable freelancer to "tweak" the content and make it your own.

- Compile multiple PLR products into one longer, full featured package.

- Create training packages - "how to" guides and courses that include a variety of training material derived from various PLR content sources (reports, worksheets, ebooks, etc.).

How you monetize PLR will depend on your target audience, your niche, and your overall goals but one thing remains the same - you can start making money from PLR TODAY even if you've never done it before!

## Quick start "prep"

Before you can monetize PLR, you need to complete a few simple steps that will not only help you make more money but will drastically improve the quality of the PLR that you distribute under your brand.

## Edit content

Even if the content is professional and well written, you will want to touch up the content in a few different ways including:

## Inject your personal message

You want your customers to feel as though the content was written for them, so it's important that the information contained within the PLR release represents your personal message and voice. Touch up the content by adding in your own introduction or add a "Note From: Your Name" at the beginning of each guide.

## Inject your brand

If you are planning to use PLR to create information-style products for your business, it's important that each release carries a strong brand message. It's important to remain consistent with every product you release under your company, and this may include font styling's, color schemes, layouts, templates and even chapter titles or headlines. Run through each PLR product quickly and make sure that it reflects your company and the impression you wish to make.

## Inject your links

If you plan to monetize PLR content or use it in giveaways, incentive offers or lead-in free products that capture attention and push your marketing message out to your audience, it's important that you include direct links to your websites and blogs.

Every PLR product could be used as a lead generation tool or a traffic magnet, so take the time to add in relevant links that direct readers to other useful resources.

## Inject your sign off

Consider creating your own 'sign off signature' and add it to all of the PLR products you intend to use, in both your product line and marketing campaigns. This may be as simple as your full name, a slogan, message of encouragement or a logo.

When editing content, you will also want to consider restructuring chapters and re- titling Table of Contents to make it your own. Since PLR is sold to multiple buyers, changing things up just a bit will help prevent refund requests from customer's identifying the material as PLR (or as being sold by other people).

Sometimes spending just a few minutes editing, tweaking, and improving the content and layout, can do wonders at adding incredible value to the PLR products you purchase, and in transforming each one into a product that you can call your own!

## Instant monetization strategies

Once you have edited the content so that it better reflects your message and brand, the next step is to determine how you plan to use the content.

- Do you want to create your own PLR store?

- Do you want to upload PLR based products and sell them directly from your website?

- Do you want to use PLR products as incentive offers on lead capture pages?

Depending on how you plan to use or monetize PLR content – we will outline the next steps you need to take. To help you get started, here are a few ways that I instantly monetize every private label package I purchase:

## Setting up a store

Creating a digital store that offers PLR content is exceptionally easy, especially with the power of WordPress.

There are many different templates to choose from that will help you create a full featured storefront in a matter of a few minutes.

You can use a series of powerful plugins to handle the delivery and order processing.

One of the easiest plugins that comes bundled with everything you need to set up a fully loaded e-commerce shop is found at getshopped.org

Get Shopped offers a full payment gateway while providing instant protection for all digital products, making it easy to set up a digital storefront in minutes.

If you already use a payment processor or product protection service such as e- junkie.com or DLGuard.com, you can easily integrate payment links into a blog- based eCommerce shop and let your preferred processor handle payments and delivery. If you aren't currently using a digital delivery system, you may want to take a look into digitaldeliveryapp.com, a fully loaded payment processing and delivery system that will automatically process orders, deliver digital files and even subscription-based offers.

When looking for a commerce friendly template for your WordPress storefront, I recommend choosing a 2-column theme that is clean and simple. You want potential customers to find the kind of products they are looking for quickly and easily, without having to fumble through a complicated navigation system, so keep your blog free of clutter, and limit ads to just 2 or 3.

You can browse through 20 of the best WordPress eCommerce themes from webdesignledger.com/ resources/20-best-wordpress- ecommerce-themes or run a quick search through Google for "WP eCommerce Themes". While you can pay for a premium theme, there really isn't a need to as there are hundreds of free templates and themes that will work just fine!

You will also want to give customers the option to search through your inventory for specific product types or by category. You can download free plugins that will enable on-site search from wordpress.org/extend/plugins/wp-e-commerce/ where you will also find hundreds of other free eCommerce plugins that will further enhance your storefront options and capabilities.

Just remember that every time you enable a plugin, you run the risk of slowing down page loads, so start with only the essential plugins needed to provide your customers with a positive shopping experience.

When creating a digital storefront based around PLR products, you will want to create categories for all of the different product types and formats that you are offering.

For example, if you have PLR reports, you will create a category called "PLR Report," or you could break it down even further and create categories and sub- categories around specific topics, markets, or niches. Just do all that you can to make it easy for customers to find exactly what they are looking for.

Keep in mind that the keywords you use within your category titles will also help your website rank within the major search engines!

## Build an automatic sales machine

If you are interested in making fast cash with a "done for you" website, you will want to look into Automated Sales Websites that will do everything for you, including:

- Upload fresh content every month.

- Handle all orders and delivery.

- Generate professional sales pages instantly.

These are fully automated stores that not only create the sales system for you, but they will deliver the products to your customers every single month, leaving you free to focus on other aspects of your business!

One of the easiest, most powerful solutions available to you is found at MarketingEbooksClub.com where you'll be able to gain instant access to your very own sales site that includes:

- Customized website and sales page

- Instant products! (You will have your very own special reports to sell instantly!)

- Monthly updates - all set up on autopilot, leaving you nothing to do!

Plus, all of the products come automatically branded with your links, encouraging customers to return to the site time and time again!

Check it out at MarketingEbooksClub.com and set up your own PLR based store right now, without ever having to lift a finger. This is true automation!

## Build a PLR powered membership site

You can monetize PLR very easily with a membership-site model. Here's how it works:

You build a simple subscription-based website that offers customers access to content on a weekly or monthly basis (I always stick with monthly because from my experience they are easier to sell)

You repackage PLR content either into "personal use products" or if you are planning on reselling the PLR rights, you will want to decide on one type of package and stick to it.

Example: You could build a membership site that offers PLR to reports that come with squeeze pages, or to a business in a box package that includes everything from a sales page to an ebook. Just the same, you could start a PLR article website that offers direct access to 50 articles a month, with PLR rights.

Whatever you decide to offer is what you will need to stick with, as members will expect the same content type (and amount) every month.

Membership PLR sites usually go above and beyond by offering bonuses, extra content, freebies, and incentives that keep members subscribed to the site. Since there are so many different avenues in which a customer can purchase PLR content, you want to give subscribers a clear reason as to why they should stick with you.

You can create strong benefits easily just by offering more - for less, or by hiring a freelance writer to create small packages of custom content that are only available to your members!

Your membership site may need a specific focus, depending on what you plan to offer. If you are offering PLR rights to content, you should decide whether you are covering a wide market (such as marketing or design), or a more specific niche market (weight loss, PLR, etc.). One of the easiest ways to set up a powerful membership website is with www.MemberSpeed.com.

I've been using MemberSpeed for years and have been absolutely satisfied with it, not to mention how happy my members are simply because it's not only easy to use but you can really customize your website around what is most important to your customers.

In addition, MemberSpeed can be easily enhanced with plugins giving you the opportunity to expand your membership offer, build up a strong back-end, monetize through many different channels and much, much more. It truly is one of the most powerful, feature- rich and SIMPLE membership systems online.

## Selling PLR – No cost set up

If you can't afford to purchase membership scripts, download delivery clients or you just want to start off at the lowest cost possible, there are a few different ways to build a bare-bones website that sells PLR or PLR based products. For a Membership PLR site, if you can't afford DLG, then here's how you do it:

- Log into PayPal and click Merchant Services at the top.

- Click the Buy Now Button.

- Choose Subscriptions from the drop-down menu.

Give it an item name and customize your button - however, you want it to look.

- Enter the billing amount for each cycle, and choose what a "cycle" is

Skip the Track Inventory Feature and enter any checkout page specifics you want for your subscribers and then create your button!

PayPal will handle your subscriptions, but you'll be responsible for manually delivering via email the monthly deliverables to each PLR buyer – and make sure you do it with a BCC (Blind Carbon Copy) so that you're not showing every buyer's email address to the group.

If you don't have a website, consider using WordPress.com or some other portal such as Blogger.com, although I caution you that with free sites, you don't own the page, and it can get deleted in the blink of an eye without warning, so only use it as long as you absolutely HAVE to.

You can set up your WordPress.com site with the introduction as your short sales copy, and then use Link Lists or whatever type of module (text, etc.) that you want to showcase the different product categories that you offer.

## Essential tools

Regardless how you plan to monetize PLR content, whether you choose to create a PLR based store or you are planning to simply create information products from existing PLR content, you will want to create a web presence all your own. To do this, you need a professional hosting account.

One of the most affordable options (and the easiest to use) is available at HostGator.com.

I choose HostGator for a few reasons including the fact that they're affordable (one of the lower-cost hosting options online), reliable; have 24/7 customer support and they're VERY easy to use!

You can start out with a Hatchling Plan, but it only allows one site. It's $8.95/month. I like to use the Baby Plan for $9.95/month because it allows unlimited sites.

You will also need a domain name. One of the easiest ways to uncover great keyword-based domains is by using the free domain search tool available at InstantDomain.com

When you log into your Host Gator account, scroll to the domains area, and click Add-On Domains. You will enter the domain name without the http://www part – just yourdomain.com and then hit your Tab button – it will automatically fill in the rest before you choose a password and click Add Domain.

**Step 1:** Register a domain name that represents your offer, the type of website you are creating and the kind or products available to customers (example: highqualityplr.com, weight-lossplr.com etc.)

**Step 2:** Secure a hosting account with HostGator.com (or another provider). Link your domains to your hosting account via name servers.

**Step 3:** Use "Fantastico" to automatically install WordPress if you plan to use it as the foundation for your website or eCommerce store. Fantastico comes bundled with all HostGator hosting accounts and is a simple script that allows the instant installation of many different scripts including WordPress.

**Step 4:** Set up your FTP Client to connect to your hosting account so that you can upload files, products and customize your website with templates, themes, or plugins.

**Step 5:** Integrate your product delivery and download system. You can use a service like E-junkie.com, DL Guard, or PayPal directly. If you plan to create a membership-based website, purchase a copy of MemberSpeed.com

**Step 6:** Upload your products into categories (if building a PLR based store) and use keyword-based titles to attract traffic from the major search engines. If you are planning to monetize PLR by reselling the product only, now is the time to touch up sales copy, integrate payment links and test out your sales system. Keep in mind that you can purchase PLR packages that come with pre-written sales pages and simply tighten them up! This will save you a ton of time and money.

**Step 7:** Make Money! Tools & Resources Rebranding Tools:

- ViralPDF.com Membership Software:

- MemberSpeed.com High Quality PLR Packages:

- Master-Resale-Rights.com Exclusive Membership:

- EnterpriseMembers.com

# Chapter 13
## AUTORESPONDER METHODOLOGY

When it comes to making money in email marketing, there is one tool that is essential to your success. In fact, it's one of the ONLY tools that you need to start building targeted email lists in your niche market.

With an autoresponder, you're able to automate the entire process of building and monetizing your email lists. In addition, using this automation system, you can begin to build valuable relationships with your subscribers, enforcing a positive brand message with every email.

Without an autoresponder, you'll be stuck manually emailing a database of leads and as you can imagine, not only is that extremely time consuming but managing your list would be a complete nightmare!

You know yourself that the only way to truly maximize your income online, while minimizing your workload is in your ability to streamline your business and automate as many tasks as possible.

In order to do this, you need to be able to communicate with your audience on complete autopilot so that your time is free to spend on growing your business and your brand.

So, how can you begin to automate your list building while being able to maximize your list profits instantly? This special report outlines the key essentials to setting up a powerful autoresponder campaign that will drive in leads and affectively build a positive brand in your market.

In this Chapter we'll show you what autoresponder services are available, what your options are, and how to make the best decision based on your overall goals.

## Why you need an autoresponder

If you're serious about your online business, you know that in order to be successful and develop a business based on long-term profitability, you need to free up your time and resources so they can be better spent expanding your business.

There are only so many hours in the day and in order to dominate your market and expand your sales system, your time should be spent creating new products, enhancing your websites with additional monetization channels, and on promoting your business.

So, that leaves a very important task unfinished.

## Building your list and relationships with subscribers

This is why autoresponders are such an important part of your business. With an autoresponder, you can instantly greet new subscribers and begin the relationship-building phase, without having to spend any time doing it! Your autoresponder will take care of everything for you!

As you probably know, the top leaders and authorities in your market make their money because of ONE main component that helps them stand out and make more money than ever before.

They rely on the relationships they've developed to further their business and maximize their income. They've worked hard to build valuable relationships with their subscribers and customers, and they've done this through the use of autoresponders. Without an autoresponder they simply would NEVER have the time to expand their business!

Imagine marketing to a group of 1,000 customers by emailing each one individually. It would take hours and hours just to touch base with your subscribers and at the end of the day, chances are only a small fraction of your direct emails would ever make it to their inbox!

Now, consider the advantage of using an autoresponder service that can contact your entire subscriber base within minutes – all with a click of the mouse (or set it up on COMPLETE auto pilot and it will automatically email your subscribers on predetermined times or dates!).

Not only will you be able to stay in constant communication with your subscribers, but you'll finally be able to take advantage of "automation monetization", by combining content-based emails, which offer valuable free information, along with promotional based campaigns that trigger an avalanche of orders!

## Securing your autoresponder marketing system

You should now understand the importance of an autoresponder when used as part of your marketing strategy. So, the next step is to choose your autoresponder service provider.

While there are many different options available to you in terms of the type of autoresponder you use, it's recommended that you choose a professional account that is hosted by a third-party company.

Here's why:

Should you choose to host your own autoresponder software, you are opening yourself up to many potential problems, including:

## Spam complaints

You will have to be on the look-out for spam complaints that come in both directly, and to your ISP. Since you're hosting your own autoresponder, if a subscriber feels that you are emailing them without consent, they may contact both your hosting provider and your Internet service provider leaving you at risk of losing your accounts.

## Ensuring compliance

By hosting your autoresponder with a professional service you are guaranteed that your emails are compliant with the SPAM-CAN act of 2003.

## Higher Delivery Rates

Professional autoresponder companies are experts at ensuring high delivery so that your emails make their way to your subscriber's inbox. If you host an autoresponder on your own, you may find that your delivery rates are very low, or that your emails wind up in peoples spam folders, where they do you no good.

## Extended features

The majority of professional autoresponder providers offer a variety of important tools and resources that make it easy for you to tweak your campaigns and maximize open rates, and response rates (which equate to more money for you!).

Included with most professional autoresponder providers are tools such as the ability to split test, monitor performance, as well as the ability to segment and target different parts of your overall list. These are all important features in order to maximize your email marketing results.

There are many other reasons why a professional autoresponder service is the best choice for your email marketing, including:

## Unlimited mailing lists

With a professional autoresponder provider, you'll be able to create an unlimited number of campaigns and mailing lists, giving you the opportunity to target specific segments of your market as well as venture into as many different niches as you wish!

## Advanced segmenting

If you really want to maximize response rates, you'll want to segment your lists so that you're able to connect with specific subscriber groups. For example, if you were promoting a product geared towards beginners, you could target only those who have indicated that they are new to the business. You do this through "list segmenting", which utilizes demographics to categorize subscribers and break them down into specific, identifiable groups.

## Siphon trust & credibility

Many of your potential subscribers may not feel comfortable joining a mailing list that is managed or handled by an unknown source. People don't want their sensitive or personal information shared or distributed beyond their consent and so by hosting your mailing list with a professional and well-known autoresponder provider, you won't have to worry about potential subscribers being concerned about how their information is stored. Another consideration is whether you should pay for an autoresponder service or take advantage of free account offers.

The upside to this is that you can start building your email lists instantly without any start-up costs involved, however the downside is that with the majority of free autoresponder offers, your messages will carry third-party ads that may hinder your ability to monetize your own campaigns.

In addition, you'll put yourself at risk of not being taken seriously as subscribers will see that you are using free services, rather than a professional autoresponder account. When it comes to making money online with email marketing, it's always wise to invest in your financial future by securing a professional autoresponder account.

## So, which provider should you choose?

In the next segment, we'll take a look at the different options available to you so that you can choose the best fit for your business and budget.

## Top autoresponder providers

Choosing an autoresponder provider is an important decision because once you've begun to build a mailing list, it's not always easy to transfer your contacts over to a new provider.

While the majority of professional autoresponder providers offer the option to "export" your database of leads and then "import" them into a new autoresponder account, all of your subscribers will have to re-confirm their desire to be on your mailing list and as you can imagine, for this reason alone it won't be easy to transfer everyone over.

So, with this in mind you'll want to spend some time evaluating the top autoresponder providers online so you can make the very best choice for your future in email marketing.

To get started, we will take a closer look at how autoresponder providers differ and what they have to offer.

Keep in mind that autoresponder pricing works on a tier-based structure, where you pay based on the number of subscribers you have so as your list grows, you can expect your monthly charges to change.

Get Response, available at GetResponse.com was founded in 1998 and is a leader in autoresponder marketing. You can get in for free by taking advantage of their new account option, however for just $9.95 a month, you'll be able to grow a list of up to 250 contacts.

Aweber, available at aweber.com was also founded in 1998 and has a solid reputation within the email marketing arena as being a quality and reliable tool for marketers. With high delivery rates and extended features that include segmenting and split testing, you'll have access to all of the tools you need to maximize performance.

Constant Contact, available at ConstantContact.com offer a free trial for the first 60 days, giving you the opportunity to experience their service and guarantee of customer satisfaction with no upfront costs involved. You can then upgrade your account based on your subscriber units for as little as $15 a month.

iContact, available at iContact.com offers a wide range of features with a low monthly budget plan for beginner marketers with smaller lists. You can easily upgrade in the event your list grows quickly for as little as $9.95 a month.

Autoresponse Plus, available at AutoresponsePlus.com offers a full-scale autoresponder script that you can host on your own services for a one-time payment of just $197.00. With this script you're able to install your own autoresponder portal, with additional features included such as social media integration and link tracking.

## Moving forward

Your next step is to secure a professional autoresponder account of your own, so that you can begin to build and monetize your email lists.

Spend some time browsing through the feature overview lists on the top autoresponder provider websites and choose the provider that best suits your needs. Then, once you've secured your own autoresponder account, you'll be able to finally join the ranks of successful email marketers!

# Chapter 14
## SOCIAL MEDIA MARKETING FOR CASH

In case you're wondering whether social media could be useful for your business, the verdict is yes: social media is a great way to drive repeat business and attract new customers. Whether or not you're just starting out, this guide will help you sort out what is needed to get the business moving, and if you implement the steps outlined here, you should be able to see a positive change within a short period of time.

Social media has changed the way people connect, discover, share information, and conduct business, but you already know this, so let's get to the good stuff. Here's what you need to know:

- Social media – this is the technology people use to connect, share ideas and experiences. Businesses tap into this infrastructure to connect with customers and grow their brands.

- Social networks – such as Twitter, Facebook, LinkedIn, etc.; these are the places where social interaction take place.

- Social media marketing – using this technology to build relationships that build awareness, customers trust and of course, repeat business.

Any of this make sense? It should because social media is basically just word-of-mouth powered by technology. Over 75% of people are highly likely to share content they like online with their friends, family, or coworkers; and 49% do this on a weekly basis.

## Social media for your business

Both large and small businesses use social media to do the following:

- Promote the name of the brand and business

- Tell people about their products and services

- Find out what people think about their brand

- Attract new customers

- Build stronger relationships with existing customers

## What are the advantages of social media to your business?

There are many advantages to using social media in business, such as:

- Broader reach–you're able to reach millions of people through a single popular social media platform.

- Localized, targeted marketing–it's essential to target your niche specifically in order for the message to have its intended effect; and social media facilitates this.

- Low-to-zero cost–majority of popular platforms are free to use, and the ones that cost money won't stretch your budget thin.

- Quick and simple setup–It only takes a short time to setup an account and post information- and anyone can do it.

- Personalized communication–social media allows businesses to send personalized messages to customers and help them with common problem such as implementation.

## The setup

How do businesses use social media effectively? It all starts with goals. If you set your goals right and know from the start what you expect to achieve from your marketing efforts, it shouldn't be too difficult to organize and implement a winning strategy. These are some of the ways established brands use social media to expand their reach:

- Spreading the word–show your customers who you are, what you can do and more importantly, how your product or service can benefit the prospect.

- Drive sales–you can do this by offering existing customers special offers or starting a promotion. Just make sure they like it well enough to share it with their own social circles.

- Provide people great customer service–this is essential to any business, but social media makes it much easier to engage with customers and find out what it is they need from you. Find out what they are saying about you and establish a good feedback loop.

- Keep them coming back–when you set in place an effective system and build strong relationships with your customers, they will always come back.

## Key networks

Different types of social networks work for different marketing purposes. The key is to find a central position that takes into account as many platforms as possible, without saturating the message. Some of the main platforms include:

- Facebook – a website that allows you to have conversations with your customers and post photos, videos and news about new products and features.

- Twitter - a micro-blogging website that you can use to send and receive short messages as well as post photos.

- YouTube – the most popular video hosting website. This should be used when posting promotional videos and the videos should be linked to other social media networks.

- Photo-sharing – these are websites that allow you to store, organize and share photo collections with customers. If you're not entirely familiar with social media and don't know how you could use it to grow your business, this chapter was written for you. The specifics may seem complicated at first but it's all worth learning more.

## How to get started with social media

When using social media to grow a business, the worst action is no action, and the worst problem is invisibility- not bad perception. If you're part of the conversation you can always massage what people are saying about your brand; but if nobody knows about you, then you have no chance of growth. What this means is that you need to get involved: not only to exploit the many business opportunities available for your business, but also to develop a winning reputation.

It's a good idea to start by developing a plan that takes into account the social trends that characterize social media inter-action today and organize a framework that will help make your conversations popular and relevant. But with all this mass of social networking sites and tools available today, how does one navigate through it all to set up a strategy that works?

Here are ten steps to get you started:

## Setup goals

Think about what you hope to achieve from the social inter-action. Are you doing it to generate direct sales, offer better customer service, or better yet, develop stronger relationships with your clients? Your answers to these questions will deter-mine how you go about setting goals.

## Consider your resources

It's going to take more than a clever idea to set up a market-ing plan that works, and you need people working for you. Someone has to set up the social media accounts, engage with customers and respond to questions, create compelling content, etc.

## Know your audience well

Find out where your audience spends time, what conversations they are involved with, who influences them, and what kind of information they're looking for from you. In order to provide your audience what they want, you first have to understand who they are, how they think, and what they want from you.

## Come up with good content

Once you find out what your audience is into, you can then work on giving them something to talk about and possibly share. Conversations have to keep going and this means creating lots of good content for the audience. Try to create a variety of different types of content that can be shared.

## Consider quality

While the pressure of creating content is certainly understandable, you cannot resolve to create a bunch of pointless topics for the sake of interaction; people will get tired of it. The goal here is to build actual customers, and that won't happen if you're not offering useful information and products/services.

It's tempting to promote your products every two minutes on every social platform available to you, but you may need to do something not self-promotional so that you don't come off overly self- absorbed or too salesy.

Find time every day to look up what's going on in social circles and engage with your customers to find out what the general vibe is about your brand.

Learn the culture of social networks. What are your competitors doing and what does that teach you? Learn more about social trends and find out where companies or brands have gone wrong with marketing strategies so that you don't make similar mistakes.

Acquire brand ambassadors by observing the most active people in the social networks and encourage them to sell your brand. So which social platforms should I concentrate on? Most large brands operate dozens of social media accounts but they have more people working on that so you might not be able to start big. Besides, you want to learn how to use each website perfectly to get your message across and this might take more time if you embarked on creating 20 social media accounts at once. Focus your attention where it matters and learn everything about those websites and how larger businesses use them to promote their own brands.

## Facebook

When it comes to this, the numbers don't lie; you want the websites with the highest number of active users in order to get a broader reach. Facebook alone will get you access to a social network with over a billion users worldwide. If Facebook were a country somewhere off the coast of California, it would be the third largest in the world in terms of population. Features such as Like, Timeline, Newsfeed, Apps, Cover Photo, and Mobile Upload; these will be useful as you gradually build a connection with your prospects, so learn the lingo and get to work.

## Twitter

You get up to 140 characters when sending out messages to your subscribers and you can include links, videos, and photos as well. Adding images and videos expands the message because the words are somewhat limited, and you need to communicate more effectively than 140 characters can articulate.

If you have an existing Twitter account for your brand but have let it drop off lately, you might want to take a fresh look at what Twitter's offering. Features such as real-time marketing and multi- screen usage will be useful to your marketing efforts. In the world of micro-blogging, Twitter stands as the most powerful tool you can use for business. Other popular micro- blogging sites include Plurk, FriendFeed and Tumblr.

## Present your brand

Your social media accounts form the foundation of your marketing efforts. They give you the chance to tell the world about your business and so they need to be well defined. Create a web presence people find appealing and distinct; that way people recognize your brand across multiple platforms.

In order to present the brand more confidently, you have to fill up and complete the profile, and make sure people know your bio, the actual location of the business and the address to the official company website. When creating a social network for your business, start with these people:

- Customers

- Business partners, suppliers, and contractors

- Relevant trade organizations for your industry

- Local businesses in your neighborhood

## Work up a time schedule for social media

You could end up spending hours each day trying to keep up top speed with what's going on online so if you want to manage your time better, create a time management structure to keep your time online useful and strategic. One way to do this is to find out what time your customers start responding to your feeds and take a couple of hours to engage.

## A social media marketing plan for your business

Effective social media strategies require proper planning and execution. If you're new to this and expect to see results from a few blog posts and random updates, you might find the whole endeavor very disappointing. Serious marketers know that in order to harness the full potential of social media one has to incorporate at least these three elements:

- Listening to the audience

- Sharing relevant messages

- Enabling the audience to share the message

So what is it that you're supposed to share? Good content. You can't have effective social media marketing without good content. The entire marketing plan originates from a solid content creation strategy. The good thing about useful content is that it gets people to appreciate your brand and share; and the sharing is what builds your brand.

This works whether you're a small business or a large multinational and it costs very little to set up so the budget shouldn't be a major factor when setting up. Ever heard that saying that goes "failing to plan is planning to fail?" It's very true when it comes to marketing because creating a well- detailed social media strategy is just as crucial as having a rock-solid business plan.

In order to attract, engage and ideally convert fans and followers into customers, employ this strategy.

## What should I aim to achieve from social media?

This depends entirely on what type of business you're in. you may want to use it to gain exposure for your brand or simply to interact with customers because it's good for business. Remember, if you're just winging it your audience will know and that's not good for you. Try to understand your customers' goals and find out how to connect with that. One way to do this is to find out how you can use social media to solve your customers' problems.

## Who should set up the company's social media account?

For smaller companies it would be better to delegate the task to a staff member who has experience implementing effective social media campaigns. Larger companies give the job to qualified workers in the marketing department and if the budget allows, some may choose to hire a consultant or firm.

## Should I create accounts on all social media platforms when starting out?

As a starting point, it would probably be better to operate with a presence on one or two social networks and a blog. The network you choose will be determined by where your audience hangs out; so survey your customers and find out what their most popular platform is. The more the business grows the more social networks you can get into.

## What's the best social network for a small business?

Whether you're operating a large or small business, you can never go wrong with a Twitter account. The platform is easy to learn, and it gives your business a voice in the micro-blogging world. Another crucial network to be on is Google+- if only to boost your site's search engine rankings. If however, you have a B2B firm, social networks such as SlideShare and LinkedIn would be great places to reach influencers, and you wouldn't go wrong with Facebook and Pinterest.

## What's the right frequency to post updates?

Two-five posts each day should be enough. Remember your followers visit social media websites at different times, and a single post each day couldn't possibly be enough simply due to differences in timing. To reach more people, stagger the posts consistently throughout the day.

## What type of content should I post?

Again, the purpose of your marketing campaign will determine what you post. But also, the platform you're using matters to a certain extent. For instance, Pinterest and Instagram are inherently visual, so striking, memorable images detailing your products and services would be ideal if you're operating such accounts.

Company events and a few behind-the-scenes photos are great for connecting with audiences on these networks. But you may also post text updates on Facebook and have them trend well, especially if you're posing a question or giving out relevant information. When using Twitter, try to keep a balance between tweets and re-tweets. Curate a diverse mix of content (photos, links, tips, short videos, thoughtful questions, etc.) across different platforms in order to keep things fresh and interesting.

## Is social media a good platform to provide customer service?

Social media has over time become one of the most popular platforms for businesses to interact with potential and existing customers. You can use all the popular platforms to respond to customer questions and complaints, order status enquires, etc.

## How exactly does one convert followers into customers?

There aren't any surefire tactics to get fan's dollars, however some tricks seem to work better than others. For example, Facebook ads are a simple, affordable way to expand your fan base, boost engagement and collect sales leads. It's entirely up to you to convert those leads. One of the best ways to go about converting leads is to implement a cross-platform contest that integrates all the popular platforms and perhaps offer sweepstakes that resonate well with the audience and draws in potential customers.

For instance, in order to drive consumers to your online store, you could send a simple tweet that describes an ongoing contest on your Facebook account and drop a link to the rules of the contest and the entry form on your online store.

## How do people go about measuring the success of their marketing efforts?

It's very important to make sure you always track your marketing metrics so as to establish which tactics are working and which aren't. Some platforms come with their own metrics; Facebook for instance gives you administrator access where you can check out page insights data and use the data to evaluate what's working and plan your future posts.

LinkedIn offers similar analytics which are essential for business pages. Google analytics can be used to measure the effectiveness of social media campaigns and see how your strategy's driving your traffic to your online store.

## Biggest mistake to avoid

You can't afford not to have a social media plan, so create one and stick to it. Remember social media is constantly evolving and in order to stay ahead you have to be prepared to adapt and redefine your strategy as needed. If you do this every few months, you will identify which tactics are redundant, and in the process, work out the best plan for your business.

Most organizations begin their social efforts by listening and engaging with their customers across different platforms, but at some point, they have to look at the staffing required to carry out an effective campaign and ask what it is they're really getting from social interaction. In order to maintain a social business strategy that binds desperate efforts together to create a long-term plan that keeps the business growing, significant time and resources have to be set aside.

## How to build brand awareness using social media

So you've already built a pretty impressive social media engagement campaign for your business; but how do you know you're doing it successfully? Keep in mind the number of followers you have doesn't always determine the effectiveness of the campaign- it's about how many people in your circles who actively respond.

There's a wide range of responses you could get from social media aside from the usual customer questions and complaints. Aside from the comments, blogs, dialogue, and re-tweets, look into this:

- Humanize the brand

- Manage perceived reputation

- Generate leads

- Create a few brand advocates

- Resolve problems with customers

- Handle crises effectively

It doesn't matter where the conversation is at:

Whether you're on Facebook, Twitter or your blog, there are a number of ways you can generate good conversations. These conversations will solidify your relationships and fans will experience a more direct connection with your business, which is what your aim is.

## Engagement for creating awareness

One common purpose of social media is to create a public profile. Consider Canadian Olympian Sarah Wells; she started a campaign on Twitter where she hoped to engage Olympic fans and raise awareness of her quest for the gold, and possibly gain a significant number of followers. Just days into the campaign, Sarah had hit the 400-follower mark, owing to the strength and enthusiasm of her friends and family. It's one example of an effective grassroots social media campaign.

## The benefits of creating brand awareness

One of the many benefits include measurability. Consider these key awareness metrics:

- Share of conversation–this is about how often you get mentioned in context of the conversations that are relevant to you.

- Share of voice–how often are you covered or mentioned in comparison to your competition?

- Mentions per time period–this describes how many times audiences discuss your brand in a given time period. It gives you a sense of overall chatter and awareness.

- Potential reach–followers, fans, or eyeballs; this is seen as potential reach because those people won't pay attention to you simultaneously.

- In bound links–an indicator of audiences that are aware of you and are talking about you. To get a better sense of which types of media drive consistent attention to your brand, look at all the active social media accounts.

## Offer people choices

Perhaps Twitter does not reflect your communication style and you prefer Facebook instead. Learn how your audiences like to communicate and give them different choices by creating more than one social media platform for dialogue. Ensure that you post the same information-perhaps in different contexts-across all platforms in order to get a response. Tools such as Hootsuite will save you a lot of time when you want to manage and schedule posts across all platforms.

Whatever channel you like most, remember to give the audiences a 360° look at your company and brand. Use a communication style that's consistent with the brand so as to avoid confusion. You will be able to build those strong meaningful relationships with your audience if you learn how to initiate smart dialogue across all platforms.

Generally speaking, people enjoy being part of a business or brand that is actively building an engaging community and multiple studies have revealed that customers prefer to purchase from businesses that have active social media pages. That emotional connection with prospects is what builds a positive business reputation.

Recognize community strength as a powerful force for a brand and employ all the features of social media in creating a massive community of happy and loyal customers.

## Lessons in brand awareness

Branding tactics keep changing and marketers have had to learn an entirely new playbook- a playbook that keeps evolving with new social platforms and technologies to make it all work. Learn what you can from larger brands that have successfully implemented their social media campaigns and established themselves as trendsetters. Each one of those large companies dominating social media today started small. YouTube was started by two friends in a small room above a pizza place and M&S begun as a market stall so don't let the competitiveness wear you out; little can still get pretty big.

## Lesson 1: Think like a publisher

Innocent founder Richard Reed adopted the publisher model of marketing by publishing multiple recipe books as a way to expand their growth. It has had a tremendous impact on the company's overall reach and also, it changed the general perception about the company- people don't see Innocent as a brand trying to sell products for cash; they're seen as a healthy company that encourages people to live healthier lives.

They also have a blog on which they post content that helps people make decisions that impact their lives positively, and this enables the company to engage with large audiences. In addition, 10% of Innocent's profits go to charity, so the blog is also used to show how they are making a difference the world over.

## Lesson 2: Find your tone of voice

When you find a tone that works for your audience, stick to it, and maintain it when creating content for all your platforms. You are marketing to people; not robots, so start by creating buyer personas and learning what their goals are and what types of challenges they face. It will help you get a better understanding of who your audience is and that way you can adjust your tone of voice to one that they can relate to.

## Lesson 3: Make your content shareable

When you create valuable and engaging content it makes you a great resource to your audience. Give your prospects what they need, and it will help create an organic audience who engages with your company and follows you across multiple platforms. Always consider how shareable your content is. Just ask yourself whether or not you would find it engaging enough if you were the audience, and whether you would consider sharing it with your own circles. If the answer is no, then you need to go back to the drawing board and figure out where you went wrong.

## Lesson 4: Create headlines that attract people

When you're trying to come up with something that will get you maximum exposure, you have to nail the headline. Most successful brands come up with dozens of possible headlines for each piece of content then settle on the one they believe would get the best response. If you can come up with something that grabs people's attention, it will expand your brand's reach and make your content that much more popular.

## Lesson 5: Never be boring

This goes without saying but you'll be surprised how many brands keep posting the same dull material on social channels. In order to ensure that your customers don't opt out of your social networks, you will have to come up with content that's not just interesting and shareable but remarkable. The only way this could happen is by making sure you don't create the same content as everyone else in the industry. Make the brand stand out in a way that makes it unique and original.

Want to show off the personality of your brand, do something quirky and experiment with infographics, videos and other visual content and see what you come up with. Keep in mind that 90% of all information transmitted to the brain is in fact visual, and the brain processes visuals 60,000 times faster than plain text.

## Lesson 6: If possible, hire journalists

Whether they're working in-house or for a large traditional media outlet, journalists have the same job; figuring out how to come up with the next interesting story that will make people want to read about. The best journalists ask questions and challenge common assumptions, and not just in terms of what business your company is into, but also other people in the same industry. That's how great content comes about, and people can't help but share it.

## How to get more engagement from your followers

As we mentioned previously, follower count is worthless in and of itself and if you believe that follower count is a badge of honor or some sort of powerful status symbol, then you've got the whole thing wrong.

But that being said, getting more followers is good for you and here's a good reason why:

The more followers you get, the more engagement you have. It's an obvious benefit to have a large number of people following you because then there's the likelihood that someone will see one or two things they like and share it. It's a math game: if more people see the content, more people will interact and share it. This means more likes, more re-tweets and comments, etc.

Such growth can provide you with excellent feedback for future discussions. If for instance one particular subject of discussion happens to get more interaction, then it could inspire you to create more content around the subject in order to keep the conversation going. On the other hand, if a customer asks a question about your brand, it could inspire you to write a new blog post.

People absolutely love to share content they find interesting and engaging. Want your brand name to be recognized the world over? It won't matter if your initial plan was to simply generate more sales for your business; social media opens up a bigger aspect of business success: brand recognition. When you set up a good campaign, you will have the opportunity to not only increase sales, but also create brand awareness and a strong sense of loyalty from customers. Let's look at ways you can increase engagement across the two most important social platforms for your business.

Twitter offers you a great platform for engagement but how much do you really know about Twitter?

Let's look at a few statistics you could find useful to your campaign:

- Engagement for brands is higher by 17% on weekends. Clearly not many people realize this, which is why only 19% of brands actually send out tweets over the weekends. Are you trying to get your audience to engage more but don't feel like working over the weekend? You could use Buffer to schedule the tweets and have them sent out while you stay cozy at home.

- Tweets with images and links get twice the engagement so work on creating photo stories that will get people talking.

- Keep your tweets relatively short. Statistics show that tweets with more than 100 characters spark fewer conversations, so work within that 100-character limit. If you've got links in the posts, it shouldn't go over 120 characters.

- The fastest-growing demographic on Twitter is 55-64 years old. If your brand accommodates the senior crowd, then it would help to reach out to the new users who are more than willing to try out new discussions and check out brands.

- Hashtags inspire more engagement. But that being said, keep the engagement at a minimum: 1 or 2 hashtags will increase engagement by up to 21% but too many hashtags will kill the conversation before it starts.

- Target mobile users. Mobile users make up 6.66% of user- generated tweets that mention specific brands so it would be a good idea to link out to usernames of people you mention on Twitter and add in a hashtag.

- Mobile Twitter user's are181% more likely to login during their commute. When sending out content, think about where most of your audience could be at that time. If it's morning on a workday, then they might be commuting to the office, and it's a good time to start engaging with them; that way you can have their attention for the rest of the day. Find something interesting to occupy them in their morning commutes and they will make it a habit to check out your posts each morning.

- You want more engagement? Ask people to re-tweet. You may have heard that the best way to get your content re-tweeted is to ask for it: well statistics show that spelling out the word "re- tweet" actually increases the chances of it happening by 23 times, as opposed to abbreviating with "RT".

- Include more links in your tweets. Just like images, links are more likely to cause an effect; however, unlike images, which directly boost engagement, links tend to increase the number of re- tweets.

Now let's look at Facebook and what makes a good engagement campaign in that platform. There are a few effective strategies you could implement in order to get your followers talking.

- Create open loops on some of your posts. An open loop is where you give a hint to what's in a new post. It's actually quite simple; let's say for example you want to post an article about "Why All Business Should Use Social Media", you could just put in something like "Great post, useful guidelines", or something similar, but it wouldn't get that much attention. But if you said something like "The second point is insane! I need to implement it right now", or something similar, you would get a better response because people will want to know what the excitement is about.

- Mix up the content a little bit. If people have gotten used to you publishing blog posts every day, it's going to get boring pretty fast, so every once in a while, get them off guard and publish video series, images, podcasts, slide-show presentations, etc.

- Use older content that new audiences might have not seen yet. If you have some good material from a while back and you've accrued a significant number of new people on Facebook, consider posting one or two good stories at least once in a while. Because a larger part of your audience is new, this will add value. And for the rest of audience who might have seen the post the first time but forgot about it, this would be a great way to spark new discussions.

- Check out Facebook insights to find out which posts your followers liked the most and if you find that people respond more to a specific type of post, then you want to work on perfecting that format and find more related topics to discuss.

- Add more apps to your page. There are a variety of apps available for you depending on what industry you're in and how you want to engage with your audience so head over to the apps section, shop around and find an app that makes sense for the followers.

- Upload videos to your Facebook page and stop copying and pasting YouTube video URLs. There's nothing particularly wrong about pasting video links to other sites on YouTube, but statistics have shown that these types of videos get significantly less engagement than when users upload the videos directly. When you upload videos alongside cool posts, it allows people to interact without having to leave the page. It's a little trick which requires more effort, but it can get you more engagement in the long run.

That's where you need to start if you want to get more engagement on Facebook and Twitter. Hopefully this gives you some perspective on how audiences operate on other social networks. Companies have been investing more money in paid content distribution on Facebook and that's certainly a viable option for when you want more targeted ad campaigns and great content, but if that's not part of your strategy, you can still achieve solid engagement with these strategies.

## How to get more fans to your Facebook page

Has your Facebook page growth been stalled? Now might be a good time to start evaluating your Facebook strategy, see what's working and what isn't, and cut out whatever's stalling growth. Let's start with the basics: a lot of people get impressive engagement on their personal Facebook profiles and while that's a good get in itself, it's still important to set up a business page.

If you're creating products, offering a programs or services, your business page will allow you to create an image that will allow you to become an authority on the subject and once you get to that place, you can then discuss your business freely. It should be your goal to become that go-to authority in your niche and that's why you need to have a business page.

## Set up a marketing plan to get you more fans

Start with these three phases when putting together the plan:

- Attraction-this means finding different ways to grow your fan base depending on what they're in too. Learn as much as you can about your audience and create a persona of your typical fan. That way you know how to center the campaign around them.

- Promotion—come up with strategic posts and keep them short and to-the-point.

- Sales—one of the best ways to get audience feedback for when you want to sell products and services is to ask questions. You'll find out what your audience wants and develop something they will spend money on.

Now in the next step you can use the following tips to really grow your fan base.

## Connect with fellow page managers

So let's say you run a small ice cream store and have already set up a Facebook page with a decent following: try to make a live connection with the pizza parlor across the street if they attract the same clientele. Talk to the owner and invite them to do a little cross promotion on Facebook, where you can share posts with your audiences and forge stronger connections.

## Share content

This works across all social platforms because when people see and share your content, it has a direct impact on your sales. Have you considered taking original photos and using them as part of your content on Facebook? It could be a simple behind-the-scenes picture at your workplace, a thought-provoking image, or an inspirational picture: whatever you decide to post should serve to get people sharing. Just make sure to follow copyright laws when downloading pictures online.

## Tag your Facebook page on your personal profile

The goal here is to make sure your prospects can access your page easily. Pages aren't getting too much attention these days so you need to come out and make sure to tag your business page so that people can like it right from your update.

## Link the page to your profile

It's a simple thing to do but a lot of businesses get it wrong. If users can search and find your personal Facebook page, then you want to make it so that your business page is just as easily accessible.

## Include Facebook in your email signature

Do you send out emails every day? This is not a complicated trick: just a reminder to include a link to your Facebook page in your email signature. Use a mail program that allows you to customize your email signature and put in clickable icons.

## Comment on different pages

This is yet another great way to get more people to notice you on Facebook. Find out which other pages your audience could be having conversations and get involved. Like complementary Facebook pages as your own, and then keep an eye on your home page feed and respond to the posts.

## Run contests

Lots of businesses do this just to get more likes on their page. It will cost you to run a contest but hopefully you've set aside a marketing budget for this campaign. All the contests have to be run through Facebook apps but they don't cost too much and they're relatively easy to set up.

## Set up a QR code for your business card and use the link for your Facebook page

Websites such as QRStuff and QR Code offer the codes for free so set up the codes on any of your business cards so that people can find you.

## Use a sponsored like story to generate more fans on Facebook

There are many ways to advertise on Facebook these days and one popular option is the sponsored like story which advertises your page to your fans' social networks, basically notifying their own friends about your page and showcasing that the user's friend already likes your page.

## Include a like box on your site

If your website gets a good amount of traffic, you should be able to get a fair number of likes on your page. Track where the likes are coming from and find ways to win more fans from those avenues.

## Use blog feeds

Apps such as RSS Graffiti and NetworkedBlogs can be used to import posts from your blog and right into your Facebook page. Make sure the posts are useful to your audience and keep it engaging so as to enhance interaction.

By now you've probably heard that offering your Facebook fans something extra can be an effective way to grow the number of fans you have. It's simple, you come up with an offer you know people will love, spend time promoting it through all your social channels, and in the process, get more people coming in on your official Facebook page.

For many businesses, special offers are a regular component of their marketing strategy. Things like special discounts, coupons and giveaways are used to attract new customers and reward the most loyal. But sometimes creating this type of campaign is not as effective as one would hope, and prospects remain unmoved.

In such cases, a downloadable content campaign would be a great solution. If for instance you run a restaurant, you could offer your followers a recipe for the upcoming season. Likewise if you're a marketing consultant you could offer a white paper with helpful tips for prospects and clients to enhance their marketing efforts. It is a way to showcase your expertise and also build familiarity and trust, which will be crucial to your own growth.

## Examples of businesses using social media successfully

Are you experiencing the success you thought you'd have with social media? Or could it be that your business has seen little-to-no growth even after rolling out a bunch of campaigns to get the brand noticed? If you've had some bad luck with social media, then you're certainly not alone because many companies, both large and small, experience some sort of difficulty achieving their marketing goals at some point, but what sets some of them aside is the fact that they learn fast, and adapt.

Look at some of the tactics used by companies that employ effective social media strategies: don't focus too much on their target audience, because that's hardly relevant. These tactics will work on just about any audience if done right.

## Martell home builders

This is an Atlantic Canadian custom home building company which in the past relied on realtors to keep the business afloat. This however changed once they decided to embrace social media and they finally developed an effective direct-to-consumer strategy which kicked out the middleman and allowed them to bring in the business.

This all started with the creation of a blogging strategy that mainly focused on giving homeowners and would-be homeowner's valuable tips about home ownerships and they were able to capture the attention of countless homebuyers. Posts such as "Home Staging Tips and Techniques" were particularly useful to their audience and today, the company gets 86% of their total leads from consumers.

An important point here to note is that multiple studies have revealed that people respond more to blog subscription via email as opposed to RSS feed. Martel clearly understands this as seen on their call to action which reads "Get the blog sent to your inbox." It's a smart way to get new leads while making sure to maintain value by giving out new blog updates.

Another feature the company executes well is customer service, especially where they take advantage of modern geolocation technology by mounting trackers on contractors' vehicles, so that customers know exactly where the contractor is when on the job. It eases the customers' minds and makes it look like the company understands their customers perfectly.

With such innovative technology and profound understanding of their customers, Martell has been able to grow their brand beyond what anyone could've expected, and they have made the homebuilding experience a social thing. They also have photo galleries showing clients' homes under construction which allows people to monitor closely the progress as the house comes to be. It's one of the most shareable contents on their website because clients get to share the images in their own social circles, with friends and family.

Another feature Martell uses for social integration is the Facebook like box, which is updated dynamically every time a user visits their page on Facebook. It's a nifty little widget which shows how many people liked your Facebook page and also displays faces of some of your fans. One advantage to using this feature is the fact that people can join your fan group without having to leave your website. It compels visitors to stay longer on your website and that in itself increases your fan base significantly.

Tip: When creating your own strategy, try to think outside the box like Martell did by giving their clients access to unique photos showing the construction of their homes and allowing them to track their contractors' whereabouts.

## Zappos

This is a popular online retailer that focuses on clothing, shoes, and accessories. Zappos is known mainly for the great emphasis they put on building strong relationships with their clients. The company's Facebook tab reads: "Let's be in a Like-Like relationship." It's one of the ways they show real commitment to their fans, and this helps solidify trust with their customers.

The company's attraction process involves those asking people to Like them and then join their email list. When a visitor clicks the like button, they bring up a sign-up page where people can join the community and get access to products. Because they wait until a visitor joins the community, it gives people a sense of value and it shows they actually care about getting to know their fans and building relationships.

Zappos also uses another interesting strategy where they reveal certain content to fans only. It's actually called "fans-only content" and it encourages people to join in so they can access things like cool fashion images, videos, and insider tips. The process is as simple as clicking the like button and the company gets new people coming in every hour, joining the special community to be a part of a fashionable and well-informed group.

Zappos has a custom welcome tab which features comment widgets, where fans can talk about products, and the posts appear on their own pages or profiles telling their friends about Zappos products and what they like most about the company. It is a great strategy for social proof.

As far as engagement strategies go, Zappos doesn't hold back with their "Fan of the week" contest where they have fans send in their pictures with the Zappos box, and other fans get to vote for the picture they like most. The winner gets their photo posted on their wall image where everybody can see. No doubt the company puts their fans first.

Tip: Find out how you can use the power of social media to make your fans feel like stars, and they will love you for it. Shine a spotlight on your followers on all your social media channels and they will be compelled to talk about your brand. It doesn't take a multi-million-dollar strategy to be able to do this; just borrow a few ideas from what Zappos and other brands are doing and mold your own strategy to be more effective but still affordable.

## Giantnerd

Giantnerd sells equipment designed for outdoor activities such as biking, hiking, snowboarding, etc. This company has in place one of the best examples of social media interaction in the industry. It works by offering fans friendship while also giving them the best value in the process and they've also merged their website with social media in every aspect.

The official company website features a custom social network that requires a single click to join and makes it very easy for visitors to join. Another cool feature is the incentive program which offers new members a 5% discount on products—they call it the Nerd—save 5%" promotion and it pulls in a significant number of new members.

Giantnerd saw their average order grow by 50% after they put up the like button, a major ROI boost from social media. In addition, they provide a bunch of ways for customers to find information when researching products on their website. For instance if a potential customer wanted to find information on a specific product, they could check out feedback from other social buyers; perhaps log in to the company's WikiNerdia, and get to see all the different products available, including photos and descriptions.

With this great solution for interaction, customers are able to ask important questions about different products by posting on the board for the rest of the community to comment. A lot of studies have shown that people trust their friends and fellow consumers more than they trust the brand, and so it's crucial to have a forum where customers can interact and discuss products as they learn more about the company.

## Social media marketing mistakes to avoid

What common mistakes do small-scale business leaders make when implementing their social media strategies? There are quite a few and we're going to look into it so that your strategy comes out solid.

Thinking of social media implementation as a sprint instead of a marathon. A lot of people expect the job to be quick and simple but that's not the case. You can't get into it and commit a month to social media then step back and hope it all works out in the end: the entire plan will fall by the wayside, and you won't have anyone to blame but yourself. Give it time to grow and be there to make sure you adjust the details of your plan as needed. Remember you are building relationships –so commit at least a year to engagement and advertising before you can expect to see real traction.

## Not having a strategy

This would have to be the biggest mistake anyone could make when running any type of business. Have a clear strategy and understand why you are using it and what you expect to get from it. Also, keep tabs on the movements on your social platforms to make sure you're on track and have what you need to support the totality of your efforts just in case you need to protect the entire campaign from being disjointed.

## Not listening

Just because you have good content and can keep your audiences engaged indefinitely doesn't mean you should go out on a relentless rant about whatever you think is important. The core of what you're doing should be to make connections; and, just like what happens in the real world, (away from the internet) people will like you more if you seem to listen to their rambles and want to help them. If you're constantly talking and not paying attention to the feedback, then you'll miss out on a great deal.

## Posting bad feelings

This happens more times than you'd imagine. A few CEOs have resulted to using sites like Twitter to air their bad feelings, starting pointless arguments with competitors, workers, etc. some people go as far as posting derogatory language and that's about as low as anyone can get. Try to remember ethics and conduct yourself professionally- that way people will respect you and you won't have to worry about brand image.

## Not moderating self-promotion

This occurs more in small businesses where the owners spend most of their time trying to market or promote themselves. Don't forget social media is constantly evolving; so what you're doing now might not appear to hurt your business, but your brand could suffer later on. Look at the forums and find out what the customers are saying. And don't forget about the reach you have on social media. It can take over two decades to build a business and watch it go down in 20 minutes because someone wasn't paying attention.

## Unrealistic goals

You cannot expect social media to run your business entirely. It's not the only way to get results so polish up the other tools you have in your arsenal and see how you can compart-mentalize. Whatever plans you come up with, ensure you set reasonable expectations for your team.

## Not making the posts relevant to the customer

Nobody wants to receive 20 tweets a day hearing about you. People want messages that are relevant and of value to them. So give them something that's going to be interesting, useful, and shareable: but don't send too many messages because you don't want the consumer annoyed. Keep the messages short, succinct and of value to the consumer.

## Not responding to fans

Common mistakes here are:

- Ignoring customers

- Not updating content

- Bad design and branding

- Not responding to or addressing comments and complaints

- Spending too much time working on promotional material

## Not understanding personal and professional lines

If you're using your Facebook page to post professional material about your business, try not to make it a platform for your other casual or personal posts. Decide whether you want an account to be personal or professional, but don't make it both. LinkedIn is a good platform for conducting business professionally, so you could set up there, and use Facebook for more personal content.

## Making casual assumptions

If you evaluate many cases of failure, much of it can be attributed to false assumptions.

Highlight these assumptions and stay away from them:

Researching and monitoring aren't important- On the contrary, it is critical to understand the way your market engages with each other and with your company. The best way to initiate customer engagement and interaction is through social media- while social media provides a good platform for businesses to engage with customers, it's not the only way to interact and it's certainly not good for every type of business, so check out your customer behavior.

It's impossible to measure ROI. There are dozens of tools you can access online for this, so don't operate under that assumption.

## A business profile is more important than a personal profile

Many companies start out by making company profiles appear as company portals, and trim them with a lot of complicated information value and relevancy. What this does is increase bounce rates because people check in and then flip out to different profiles and don't even scroll down. To avoid this, start by creating a profile that people will find interesting. Work on getting them in, engage them and then carefully start propagating your message.

## Underestimating the resources needed to put it all together

How much do you think it would cost your business to set up and maintain a decent social program? Look at the math to make sure you don't have the wrong idea.

## Failing to understand that it's all about building relationships

If you're getting into social media because everybody else is doing it and it feels as if you're getting left out, then you won't have a proper plan to succeed. It's one of the reasons people go and throw out all sorts of profiles on every social platform worth mentioning, trying to sell the brand to everyone, and hopelessly failing.

When you understand that the concept is relationship-building and give it time to grow and mature, then you'll make different choices.

## Not integrating with other social assets

The way to get the most out of social media is to integrate it with other forms of digital marketing efforts. Don't leave your Twitter account on an island and hope for the best; link the accounts together and make sure they are all tethered to email, paid ads and search, and the website.

Use this guide to help stay away from some of the more common mistakes companies make on social media and remember to use images and other visual content to help get people's attention so that you can drive the point.

## Tips to boost website traffic from social media
## Create the best content for your audience

This all starts with creating content that helps people; and it would be better still if the content excites and thrills. When you publish a great piece of content it helps get people's attention, and more importantly, it gets shared across multiple platforms and that's good for business because it spreads your message and gets people to know your brand and what it represents. So make sure your website has all the right tools to make this work.

Optimize it properly with widgets and any button that you find useful. Facebook and Twitter buttons are a must for any business but if your business focuses more on visuals, then add in a Pin It button to the images. When you publish new content start by going through all your profiles and share the new post with your audience so you can get that first wave of traffic.

## Optimize the content

It's important here to remember that only a fraction of your entire audience will actually see the content, and only a fraction of those people will share the content. This fraction is significantly lower on Facebook and Twitter so you may need to work on the content in order to make sure each post gets as many views and shares as possible. That way half your audience won't just be a statistic.

Consider the time you post the content, what day you're posting and the format in which the post goes out. When posting on Twitter, use big images and remember to post your link regularly. Facebook doesn't give you much with link thumbnails so use more images on your content and structure the content in a way that tells a story, as opposed to random thoughts or rants.

## Use the analytics tool

Google offers you an effective analytics tool under the "Acquisition" section on Google Analytics so use this tool to get a clear picture of your social engagement. You should be making decisions based on actual data; so whenever you post new content, consider how the last post faired and see how you can make more of an impact. Twitter offers an analytics tool as well, so you could use that to compare notes, or look into other tools available to you. All this information will help make your strategy better for your business.

## Share website links while posting content

At this stage your priority should be to boost engagement and build your profile. Talk directly to your customers and answer any questions they may have regarding products or services, so that over time they get to know you and build a relationship with you. Find a balance between sending links and sending content. You don't want your posts to be riddled with links- especially if you're operating outside of Twitter.

There should be a line between sharing content and pushing links. Obviously, you don't want your audience to think of your posts as spam, because once that happens it won't be easy to change that perception no matter how good your content happens to be.

## Make sure your website is included in all social networks

It should be one of your first moves so make sure when creating a new social program for your business, include the website URL in all social platforms. Have it visible on Google+, LinkedIn, Instagram, Twitter, etc. There should be a website

URL somewhere on your company page so don't forget to do that.

## Start blogging

Businesses find it challenging to drive content to their social media pages when they can't produce enough new content. The easiest solution here is to stay active on your blog post as a way to maintain a dynamic site and ensure that there's always something to talk about on social media. If you find it difficult to come up with regular written content, use videos instead. If you have a video on YouTube that you can use to increase awareness, embed it to your blog. Do the same with SlideShare, Storify and infographics. If the posts on your social media platforms can point to other useful content on your website, there are higher chances visitors will click through and become new customers.

## SEO

Your Facebook and Twitter pages could actually show up before the company website in a Google search. Make use of the About Us section to direct social media traffic to your website so that you don't miss out on potential traffic.

It's true that prospects will seek out your social media pages before they check into your website. They do this mainly to get a feel of your taste and culture before they decide to spend money on your brand; so ensure you maintain consistency across all the channels.

## Google author rank

Google appreciates quality content. When you link up with the content on your Google+, it tells Google that the blog was written by a real person who understands the subject, and the users get the message as well. In order to build trust in your niche you will have to establish yourself as an authority on a specific subject: and visitors will figure it out pretty quickly if you're just winging it.

## Review searches

You will have multiple websites doing this professionally, but it doesn't stop you from creating a section for reviews on your social media accounts. The goal is to have more people end up on your own pages when they search for reviews of your brand. That way you can then work on getting them to your website, where you've set up tools to ensure visitors want to hang around, and possibly spend money to have what you're selling.

## Geo-tagging

Because of the nature of social media and in particular its personalization features, your ability to reach your audience from their distinct location means a lot for the business and the message you're trying to pass over. For this reason, make sure to include geo- graphic location when creating your accounts. It could just land you a few people strictly based on location.

As you can see, there are many ways to get your audience working for you and to boost traffic so get to work and don't take any opportunity for granted. Just a reminder, remember to:

- Blog daily

- Be consistent with your audience

- Optimize posts to increase "stickiness"

- Be patient

## The future of social media

A lot has been said about Facebook's acquisition of the popular phone app, WhatsApp. At a price tag of $19 billion, it's definitely a historic purchase, and a few harbingers of doom suggest that it's a sign that we may be going back to the dot com era bubble. But keep in mind that this particular merger is not AOL-Time Warner or some other similar name in the industry that characterized the early 2000s; and in fact, paying attention to cash spent on any of Facebook acquisitions means missing a major point: where Facebook goes, everyone else follows.

Consider, it's Facebook's initial spread that basically made social media what it is today, and since then the company has been expanding the role of social media in the society, and in the process determining what qualifies as the norm in terms of behavior and service. Even with new competitors going head-to-head with Mark Zuckerberg, and a chunk of its younger users fleeing to smaller, more streamlined social platforms, Facebook's long shadow is still visible in the social sphere. While the company might not be the embodiment of modern development, it appears Zuckerberg recognizes companies that are, and knows which ones should be integrated into his platform.

Now, considering all that, what can this acquisition—and indeed, all their acquisitions—tell us about where social media is heading? We know at the moment that mobile interaction is defining social trends, and this won't stop so what Facebook is doing, and other social giants as well, is try to figure out what else we're supposed to do with all that functionality.

Aside from mobile purchases, Facebook understands that social communication requires constant growth and evolution. The company may be gearing towards streamlining services and privacy between the sender and receiver, much like WhatsApp has managed to do with a simple and straightforward setup. Even as Facebook creates more capabilities, they still have to offer users a simple individual app experience that works within the larger Facebook umbrella.

Other social media companies may choose to capitalize on that particular trend by working on simplicity, mobile access, and brevity. As marketers already understand, these days the reader accesses social posts on a much smaller device, and they have to adjust, so they make shorter posts. This push towards social communication could also send consumers into a more dynamic and interactive mindset, something marketers could use to their advantage by coming up with more gamified experiences. Whatever direction the social giants concentrate on, the services will have to be even more streamlined, and privacy will always be an issue.

# CHAPTER 15
## VIRAL MARKETING STRATEGY

Viral marketing is a marketing tactic that depends on people instead of the usual promotional campaigns to relay information to others. This strategy is normally used by internet marketers to promote their products or services. Like the biological virus where the term was derived, viral marketing relies on "carriers" to transmit the message quickly.

## The goal of viral marketing

The primary goal of viral marketing is to spur people to pass along promotional messages or advertising to others. These people essentially become product promoters, passing marketing information to others who, in turn, will spread the message to other individuals – all done for free!

Viral marketing first got noticed when email provider Hotmail. com used it in their marketing campaign. When the company went live online, each email message sent carried an ad for Hotmail along with a link to its website. As individuals were sending emails to relatives and friends, they were also sending out messages that promote the email service. After clicking on the link, recipients can easily sign up for a Hotmail account, and as they send out messages using their new account, the advertisement spreads throughout the world in a short time with very little effort from the email provider.

There are many examples of the primary elements of viral marketing and how they are put into play. The advertising cost is negligible. It uses common tasks to its advantage, such as sending emails. It capitalizes on existing resources, people in particular, to boost their products or services. Without being aware of it, each individual who uses the product becomes its endorser or spokesperson.

When a company goes viral on their ad campaign, their brand gets recognized and their sales go up, resulting in a better payday. The main goal is to send out viral messages that can be passed along rapidly from person to person without investing a lot of time, money, and effort.

## The tools of viral marketing

Viral marketing takes advantage of existing communications channels such as radio and television. Other strategies ride on blogs, banner ads, as well as social networks like Facebook and Twitter. Hotmail, in its case, used endorsements from other people. The biggest thing about going viral is that it can spread the message like wildfire to more people than traditional advertising.

While there are various strains of viral marketing, they all use the same basic principles.

- Incentive-driven opt-in pages offer free items for providing an email address.

- Pass-along messages can come in the form of interesting emails and funny video clips which people share and forward to others.

- Buzz marketing or gossip creates controversies about something which gets people to start talking.

- Undercover viral marketing is spawned by strange or false news items and spread by word-of-mouth transmitting the virus like an uncontrolled epidemic. Many individuals have used viral marketing effectively by transmitting their message within Facebook and other social networking sites. It is a great leap forward from the word-of-mouth concept as it uses the power of lightning-fast Internet to get the message out.

Viral marketing has recently been in the crosshairs of consumers, marketing experts and privacy rights defenders due to spam emails. However, those who have mastered the game use this strategy prudently to avoid drawing fire and ensure that the message will travel far, wide, and fast.

## The importance of viral marketing

For a business to survive in today's largely competitive environment, it must be able to stand toe to toe against its competition and be able to adapt to the constantly changing landscape. One strategy has come up as a solution for today's business demands and it is called viral marketing. Online or offline, it is essential for business as it can reach your clients faster and it doesn't require a lot of money to launch.

Viral marketing is a type of advertising campaign that relies on individuals to pass on marketing messages to other individuals, so that recognition of a product or service spreads and replicates, yes, like a virus. This approach can create a lot of positive impact during promotional campaigns or product launches.

Here are some reasons why viral marketing is important for the survival of your business.

## Viral marketing creates a buzz

Creating a buzz about your product brings a sense of anticipation in your buyers. A successful viral marketing campaign can accomplish this. The louder the buzz, the farther the campaign can spread. Messages that are of great public interest, attention- grabbing and easy to pass along will definitely help the campaign.

## It builds more credibility

As more and more people in the entire network talk about and recommend your brand, more credibility is built. This is because your company is endorsed by more and more people to their friends and close associates as your message goes viral, adding points to your credibility rating. The loud buzz that is generated will surely help boost product or service recognition.

## It is inexpensive

Viral marketing costs a lot less to launch but is very fast and effective in getting your message out to prospective buyers. It is the least expensive way to market your business because it doesn't require a large advertising budget. Blogging, newsletters, and email marketing are some of the ways to go viral inexpensively.

## It keeps your business in the green

Viral marketing helps to keep your business afloat. If your business has already earned more credibility, people will continue to patronize your brand and ensure your business stability.

## It can launch your business globally

Through viral marketing, your reputation as a reliable company can reach potential clients across the globe, enabling your company to branch out internationally.

## Viral messages are easy to share

Viral product messages are easy to share. Attention-getting videos can be easily embedded into blog posts, web pages and social networking sites.

## What viral marketing is not

Many people erroneously believe that viral marketing requires a huge budget to work. Not even close.

A traditional marketing campaign promotes a brand, singing high praises about its merits, and giving it a lot of exposure and expensive movie star endorsements. With today's consumers being skeptical about nearly everything, this may appear like a hard-sell for a weak product. All that big advertising dollars for so little gain. This is not viral marketing.

## What your message should be

The key here is to create an interesting viral message that will appeal to your market. You will naturally want to include your product here. Sure you can, just don't make it too obvious. It shouldn't appear like it's the heart of your message. Release the message virally and wait for sales to come in. Your viral message should be relevant, able to solve a problem and credible enough that people will want to share it.

## The 5 rules of viral marketing

One of the most amazing things about viral marketing is the moment when a brilliant idea takes off, it can launch a company to fame and financial success – inexpensively. People who are compelled to pass on your message drive other people to action. One individual transmits the story to another, which they pass on to yet another, and so on. This is harnessing the power of the buzz, the word-of-mouse, or viral marketing.

## Ingredients for viral marketing success

Success in this strategy depends on how you throw the right ingredient into the mix:

- Free web content which includes blogs, ebooks, and videos.

- Attention-grabbing information. It could be innovative, bizarre, amusing or features a celebrity.

- A group of people to start the fire.

- Links to your content. This is very important if you want your message to go out. Viral marketing doesn't have to be difficult.

The simple and more engaging your message is, the more widespread its pull will be. Here are some basic rules to follow.

## Make your offer appealing

Don't put cash value to your offer. Giveaways like access to online webinars, video tutorials, e-books, special reports are examples of low-cost/high-value items which can spur the recipients to take up your offer and pass the message on to others, increasing the chances of making it viral.

## Make your message easy to share

Be sure that your message, whether it's a video clip, an audio recording, an ebook, or any other media, can be efficiently and smoothly passed along to other people with a single click. Anything that slows down the forwarding of your message such as an opt-in page that captures emails should be minimized.

## Take advantage of existing communications networks

You don't need to own a chain of radio or television stations to reach out to people. Make yourself familiar with the popular and immensely effective social networks like Facebook, Pinterest, Twitter, Google Plus and other marketing platforms that will get the job done at no cost.

## Make it worth buzzing about

If you want your message to get opened, promote it as the next big thing to make it buzz-worthy. If people think that they are going to benefit from it or look good by using it, your redemption rate will skyrocket.

## Keep it short and simple

As was mentioned earlier, the easier your message is to understand, the greater the chances of it going viral. Keep your message free from fluff and go straight to the point. Due to the huge amount of information that bombard them each day, if people have to spend one more minute to decipher your message, then they'll find it easier to click out of the page and move on to other things.

Know your potential audience and how they are going to respond to a particular offer. One of the keys to capturing people's attention is to know what they want and over- deliver. When you provide them with something of value at absolutely no charge, expect a huge avalanche of response to follow. If people are compelled to pass on your message to friends and associates, then your chances of going viral is assured.

## The most effective viral marketing techniques

For a message to become viral, that is, to spread and replicate like a virus, it has to be easy enough to share, using as very little effort as possible, such as clicking on a link. The message should also be able to stand out effectively and capture the attention of readers. What's more, it should have some value to users but not necessarily in monetary terms. What is important is it has entertainment or educational value.

That being said, the next question would probably be – what technique should one use for viral marketing? There is no best answer for that question. Below are 7 very effective and proven viral marketing techniques that should be part of your marketing arsenal.

## Social networks

Hotmail launched a very successful viral marketing campaign long before social media was introduced. Today, it would be impossible for a business to achieve even a fraction of Hotmail's success without becoming active in social networks such as Facebook, LinkedIn, Twitter, and others. Bottom line is, if properly executed, social media marketing can boost your viral marketing like a rocket sled on rails.

## Article marketing

Content is king. It was then, it still is. If you are good in writing articles and can get them to be syndicated, it is not too far-fetched that some of your work can go viral. That is, of course, if they are original, captivating, entertaining or educational, and provides great value.

## Videos

You've probably heard of YouTube videos that have garnered hundreds of thousands of views just within a week of getting viral. If you can upload a video that is hilarious, bizarre, educational, or simply grabs the attention of viewers, you might just be the next YouTube sensation.

## E-Books

Ebook production started nearly the same time as the Internet. Ebooks are considered one of the best ways to go viral because they are fast and easy to create and have a large audience reach. People want to share a good reading experience. If the ebook you've written is educational and/or entertaining, original, and a hard-to-put-down page-turner, then people will gladly share it with others.

## Newsletters

Newsletters are not just a great way to keep your subscribers constantly reminded of your business name, they also have that strong potential to go viral. You can grab this wonderful opportunity and not leave money on the table. Here's how. Always write a note at the end of your newsletter which encourages the reader to share the newsletter with other people. Surprisingly, most of them will. All they need is a little encouraging to take action.

## Like, tweet and share buttons

These buttons provide an excellent and convenient way for your site visitors to broadcast your content via the social networking sites.

There are other forms of content you can use for viral marketing, but in some cases, real success comes from the way you promote your content to your target audience. However, it is truly possible, provided you have an amazing story that you can put in front of your audience, that they will respond positively and willingly share your content.

## How to launch a low-cost viral marketing campaign

It doesn't have to cost an arm and a leg to drive laser-focused traffic to your company website. Viral marketing is a low-cost yet effective tool to do just that. Here are some useful tips to help you launch a low-cost viral marketing campaign that will yield positive results.

## Write articles that promote your product or service

You can post these articles on your website as well as submit them to article directories. If people find your articles entertaining or useful, they can reprint them on their website, ebooks, e-zine, or newsletter. Don't forget to include your author resource box and the article reprint option below the article body.

If you don't like writing or just don't have the time, there are free or low-cost PLR articles you can use. However, to prevent being de- indexed by Google for dupe content, you should rewrite portions of these articles to alter their content and make them more unique as other people use these PLR articles as well.

## Set up your forum or bulletin board

Forums and bulletin boards are useful tools where people can post their comments and links on your site which can help your advertising campaign go viral. You can also embed an affiliate banner or one of your own above the bulletin board's header area.

Most hosting companies include these programs at no extra cost as part of their hosting package. Installing them can be done automatically using the control panel. Just type in your name, password, and other required information and your forum or bulletin board is ready to go. All you need to do is log in and manage it.

## Purchase the branding rights to a successfully viral ebook

After branding the ebook with your site URL and links, you can give it away to people at no charge and allow them to pass it along to others. Your ebook will be received or downloaded repeatedly by other individuals down the line until it virally spreads across the internet.

## Write your own ebook

Create an ebook and allow people to place their ads in it for free, with the understanding that they will, in return, give away the ebook to their newsletter subscribers and website visitors.

## Build your product website

If you have the experience and skill, you can build a website that promotes your product. You can also allow people to download your products for free and provide them with give-away right so they can distribute them freely to other people. This will enable your product and your links to propagate across the internet until your brand gains recognition and, as a result, pull in traffic to your website.

To make this possible, your free give-away product should carry your advertisement, or you should require product recipients to directly link to your website. They should also keep your copyright notice untampered as this is where you will include a link back to your website.

If you don't want to spend on paid web hosting, you can also use free websites like Blogger and WordPress to get you started.

## How to succeed in viral marketing using Pinterest

There's marketing and there's Pinterest marketing and succeeding in it only requires your understanding of how Pinterest can work to your advantage. This pin board-style of marketing has seen tremendous web traffic since its debut in March 2013. The photo- sharing website has, in fact, already generated more than $54 million in funding from foreign and local investors alike.

There is such excitement in using Pinterest for users when they create images and redefine them as "collections" of events, hobbies, and interests and more so when other users "re-pin" them to their own pin boards. Recipes, craft projects, gardening tools, no- rip hosiery, retro fashion, shabby chic furniture, sand art, it's an endless array of everything and anything. Connections, friendships, relationships, and collaborations have been established, and continue to flourish, because of Pinterest.

## Using Pinterest for business

Business is no exception and has steadily gained a niche in the Pinterest environment. Because it's such a highly visual medium, business has a particularly good opportunity to maximize its marketing strategies when it uses Pinterest. You just have to understand how it works to get information on what kind of content gets shared and why. Women make up the majority of Pinterest users, you have to take note of that, so technology and other traditionally "macho" interests like cars, golf, wrestling, and PC games are still in the process of garnering their shares of audiences.

Exposure is obviously what happens as you inevitably progress on viral marketing in Pinterest, that's why you have to keep on being creative. Pinterest is visual, and your content has to be more eye- catching than the other visuals, and your textual content has to be more informative, too, to capture more users of your pin board. While photography is the name of the game here, you have to go the extra mile and choose carefully on what kind of photography is most suitable for your line of business, which is, for instance, shoes.

## More than the usual marketing

Viral marketing of shoes is done by big name stores and competing with them will take more than the usual viral marketing because they already do that. Use Pinterest by scouring for great shots of shoes worn by ordinary people instead of celebrities, for example, a pair of Jimmy Choo on a little girl or a pair of Doc Martens on a grandfather.

Create your own images by taking the ordinary a notch higher to make them extraordinary and Pinterest can help you achieve that. Take a seasonal holiday, for instance, like Valentine's Day. If you're into the costume business, make the occasion to your advantage. Instead of yet overemphasizing that Valentine's Day is meant mostly for lovers, couples, and significant others, take on a stand on it and introduce love on February 14 as a universal form of affection between parents and children, between neighbors, between teachers and students or even between friends. Pinterest has hundreds of thousands of images which speak of that kind of platonic love.

## Diligent commenting

Riding on a trend using Pinterest is, of course, a trend by itself. If you want to know how to succeed in Pinterest viral marketing, all you need to do is actively share your information and connect to other social media sites like Facebook.

Likewise, diligently posting comments on your content, and on others' comments as well, will help you rope in more viewers and subsequently gain you potential customers. Because somewhere out there, someone, or a whole lot of someone's, will be people who not only share your interests but are willing to shell a few bucks to see them come true.

## How to succeed in viral marketing using Facebook

Strategy is what you apply when you want to rope in visitors to your website and teaching you how to succeed in viral marketing using Facebook can only mean that there are some factors which you have to take into consideration to achieve success.

A free product is always welcome. Whether the recipient uses it or not, a freebie is exciting to receive. And if the freebie is useful to the recipient, it attains more value and attracts attention to the product itself. An ebook, software, gift certificates, a pair of ear plugs, it could be anything that will be interesting to own or have. No strings attached, no contests, no free trials, no surveys, not even a small fee to sign up to be able to get it, just plain old giveaways.

## Getting your message across

Social networks have begun their competitive battle against traditional marketing tools like the telephone, television, print ads and billboards. Because marketing through social media is faster and can potentially reach four times the number of real time users, your first stop is going through your email contacts. On the surface, emailing each one personally and not sending them auto-generated information introducing your product will seem daunting.

But think of it from the recipient's point of view: getting an email which begins with a "Dear James," addressing the recipient in an informal, almost intimate manner, is way better than receiving something that greets the recipient with a generic "Dear Beloved Consumer," that makes even the word "beloved" sound too desperate for a sale.

## Set up another account

If you already have a Facebook account but use it primarily for social interaction, register for another account for your business and set up a business fan page to reach out to potential customers. A personal Facebook account will not be effective as a business tool because not all of the people in your personal circle are necessarily interested in your business or have need for the product or service which you offer. Do the same if you have a Twitter account; concentrate on being followed and followed by individuals already in your business niche.

Again, use your Facebook and Twitter accounts to "feel" your readers by actively interacting with them. Ask them questions regularly on topics directly related to your business, share photos and other images with them, get them to invite each other to expand into more networks, because spreading out the buzz about your business will be easier. The adage "the more, the merrier" doesn't hold truer than in this case when you know how to succeed with viral marketing using Facebook.

## Blogging your way

Start a blog on your business. If you're not much of a writer, hire people who write for a living to do the blogging for you. Make sure that your blog is updated often and take note of your readers' comments and ensure that you pay attention to their questions, if any, as well as their suggestions. Never underestimate the power of the follow up.

Readers who tune in to your blog may be repetitive but your patience in faithfully answering their queries will encourage other readers to note that your blog cares about them, even when they play like a broken record.

## The 7 most effective viral marketing videos

Knowing viral marketing using Facebook and Twitter and still other social network accounts is really just putting out informative but engaging content and images which others can see, relate to, and appreciate. And if you have a business which can maximize these visual, cerebral, and emotional results, you are halfway into generating more interest and, hopefully, more sales in the future.

Social media has become every business's dream marketing tool and there are more and more viral marketing videos coming up every day because of the proven effect that viral marketing, and videos in particular, has had on consumers over the past five years.

People use the internet for almost anything they need, a condition which most of us did not think possible ten or even 15 years ago. Today, we go online to pay our bills, buy merchandise, connect with long lost schoolmates, meet new friends, participate in conferences, watch films, listen to music, and transact business.

YouTube, for instance, has revolutionized the way of discovering new talents (think Charice or Gangnam style dancing), espousing causes (think PETA's anti-fur campaigns showing how animals are methodically slaughtered, without anesthesia, for their skins) and providing blow-by-blow coverage of news (think hostage situations and natural disasters like hurricanes, fires, and sniper battles).

## More than text messaging

Video watchers fall under the 17 to 58 age range with an even distribution of both genders and geography. In some places in the world where access to the internet is minimal, people still find a way to view the news, chat with friends, email relatives, purchase new clothes and write down a recipe by watching videos online in internet cafes or on their mobile phones. Viral marketing using video has, in fact, gained more ground than any other form of marketing, including text messaging.

Attention is what a business needs and there is no better way to capture it than a video uploaded and viewed by the more than ten million people who go online everyday looking for something new to watch. It has to be admitted, even by traditionalists of advertising, that video commercials are more effective than print ads, or even televised ads.

There are certainly more interesting things to watch online than television can ever produce, and because what television airs can almost always be aired online as a video as well, watching television has even become a so-so activity in the past couple of years.

## Being unconventional

Video marketing is definitely "it." Videos have this uncanny way of drawing attention to themselves merely by being "unconventional" and that word can have different meanings to different people. While the written word of print ads and texting stimulate the visual senses, videos cover both the visual and the auditory areas and provoke the mind even more.

When watching some of the viral marketing videos the viewer participates in the creation of images that engages the mind to think beyond what is seen. For instance, a video marketing nail art that is done with good lighting, convincing textual content, the latest music, and overall engaging approach will persuade even nail biters to grow their nails and try on some polish and eventually have the desire to have nail art done. To watch how a product works through a video online makes the viewer so interested they would want to see how that product works for themselves.

## To charge or not to charge

Promoting your business via viral marketing videos is cost effective. It requires very little or no cost to make a video and uploading it on most sites, especially the popular ones, is free. The choice is then yours on whether you want to charge people who view your video or let them watch it for free and let your product speak for itself.

You can categorize your video to ensure that it lands in your business niche and make target marketing easier for your product. Ensuring the correct category where your video will be in increases your product's visibility and availability. When choosing viral marketing videos, make sure that the category it is in can reach out to the greatest number of people who can be your potential customers.

## Viral marketing dos and don'ts

In the frenzy world that characterizes the internet, online marketing has done more for business than all the traditional approaches combined, but there are several viral marketing dos and don'ts which you must be aware of to ensure success in generating success for your business.

Relevancy is of prime significance because very few people will be attracted to what you put out if that content is not related in some way to what they are attracted to or interested in. For your content to be relevant, it has to be recognizable as important to the reader. Information about retro icons, for instance, should have updated news about what's going on in the lives of these icons or whether they are staging a comeback or lending their names to certain products (which, hopefully, is one of yours) or simply letting their fans and followers know that they are still alive and kicking.

## Getting instant customers

Another one of the viral marketing dos and don'ts is creating marketing content which appeals to the sense of humor of the target audience. So make your content funny in some way that reading or viewing it triggers the laugh button in people. Along with the humor factor, marketing your product in a shockingly attractive manner will certainly provoke people to think about it and develop their own ideas. Controversial topics which may have bearing on your product, for example, can trigger so many responses from viewers that demand for your product becomes more than the supply.

If you are trying to get people to buy your vacuum-packed fresh vegetables, use their photos side by side with photos of vegetables infested with chemical insecticides by choosing those with magnifying glasses superimposed on them. By letting people know that fresh vegetables, your organically grown, chemical free veggies, are available and do exist, by showing the kind of other vegetables there are in their chemical-sprayed appearance, you captivate your viewers into becoming instant customers.

## Basic dos

Still another "Do" is responding personally to comments and messages posted by readers or viewers. Yes, it's a lot of nitty-gritty work but a personal reply is always appreciated more than an automated response. "Do" post regularly and frequently sensibly because once you have introduced your product, people would want to know more about it, including new variants or any improvements to it, change of packaging, promos and giveaways associated with it and other updates. Do make use of social networking sites such as Facebook and Twitter but remember to register your business as a separate account. Choose what page your business is most suitable for, and, whether it is on a fan or community page, work your way from there in gathering reader- or viewership.

## Just a few don'ts

The "Don'ts" are comparatively few. Don't spam is Rule Number One. Spamming is a nuisance to email inboxes and can be so irritating that the recipient can be induced to homicidal proportions to find their email flooded with spam.

Don't neglect the Terms of Service condition of whatever platforms you are using to avoid future lawsuits or the closure of your site or the upload of your video, two vital conditions which translate to loss of business for you. If the Terms of Service include prohibition of posting photos which can be classified as soft porn, for example, don't be reckless and post half-nude images just to draw attention to your lingerie or intimate apparel product. Yes, you want to connect with people who will be potential customers, but no, you don't want sex addicts, pedophiles, and other deviants to flock to your site or watch your video, do you?

When using Twitter as a viral marketing tool, the last of viral marketing dos and don'ts include going overboard on the hashtags and tag every word, or make long descriptive tags, in your tweet. Don't. Go. Overboard. Use them wisely. Highlight keywords which are current, interesting and attention-getting so people can easily find your tweet. And unless you a real mutant like Mystique and still manage to look like the real

Jennifer Lawrence, don't use words which only you can understand or find exciting such as #100RandomFactsAboutMe.

## The biggest mistakes even experts make in viral marketing

Viral marketing is a powerful business strategy which can generate continuous sales for your business but remember that doing it right to avoid mistakes people make in viral marketing is no less important than putting out great content.

Even the most seasoned marketers can make the same kinds of mistakes over and over again yet most of these are avoidable. For the viral marketing rookie, being informed of them can cut the time, and the regret, not to mention the loss business, it will take to actually experience them.

## Timely and updated

Put information in quickly. People don't want to be kept waiting, especially for something they need to use at once. Make sure your server isn't slow or use graphics which take forever to download. Never subscribe to technical arrogance and assume that everyone has Macromedia because people who have plain HTML and text versions installed in their computers are potential customers as well.

See to it that your site or video has these versions readily available. Manually list search engines which people use to view your site. Businesspeople use search engines so much yet often don't see the wisdom in having their own sites listed on the very search engines they use. Learn about Search Engine Optimization (SEO) techniques and use them to strengthen the impact of your content and to stay "in" with the latest in viral marketing.

Choose who you partner with. Don't commit common mistakes in viral marketing by associating with spyware companies and spammers who operate profusely online because if you get involved with them as co-registrants or affiliates, you may be dragged into future lawsuits. Your product may be interesting enough but having a business relationship with people like those can lose you a substantial number of already existing customers. One questionable mailing can be enough for you to be labeled as a spammer by internet service providers (ISPs), making it hard for you to market online in the future.

## Retaining customers

And speaking of customers, your potential ones should not be given the third degree when they sign up with your website or open an account to buy your product or receive your newsletter. Your questions should never be beyond name, age, email address and other contact information of your future subscriber. And don't forget to include asking their permission to use their information for other activities which your business might have such as promotions and events.

Be aware of the right timing, because not being so means that you're either up in the boondocks where they know Eisenhower to still be the American president or you're simply "out of touch" with the rest of the world. If your product mainly caters to specialized markets, for instance, children of school age, and your product is school supplies in general, you do your sales and promotions of these in August before school starts in September and not in December when school is out for the holidays. And remember that although marketing is done most effectively and quickly online, don't fall for the biggest mistakes people make in viral marketing and stop marketing offline.

# CHAPTER 16
## WRAPPING IT UP!

You made it to the end!! I hope this book was an enlightening tool for you. Hopefully you took away some very key concepts to help you in your current business or help you get started in your very first business. Over many years in marketing, I have been very fortunate to learn, grow and profit in this business. There is no reason why you can't find the same success that I've had.

Apply the "hustle" and marketing instincts that will allow you to profit in your business. Remember, there are three components to your success: (1) continuous education, (2) sell, sell, sell and (3) take care of your leads and customers! Find the right opportunity at the right time, get with the right people and you will find that success is abound.

Now, there is one last thing for you to consider. This component has been one of the biggest keys to my success. Having a coach, mentor, business partner or just a friend to bounce ideas off of is vital to the success of your business.

No successful entrepreneur or successful company has been built without the help of a trusted advisor, business partner, mentor or just a friend. This is important for one very simple reason. Just because you think something is a good idea doesn't mean that it is. I can recall many times when I thought I had a good idea for a new product or marketing strategy, but my mentor would eventually say, "that won't work." Very irritating at times but it's good to have someone that has been there, done that in your corner. This keeps us accountable as business owners and prevents us from making very costly mistakes.

So I challenge you to put all these resources to good use and apply them in your marketing. Business loves speed and so does money. This is why you have to get off your butt and stop talking about making money and take action. If you do not like your current outcome in life than it is time to change those outcomes with a new course of action. If you implement the information from this book, work hard, remain dedicated to your business, and face challenges head on with action than you to will be well on your way into successful entrepreneurship.

## Stay In Touch and Join Our Team

If you would like to explore more "free" online marketing training than visit our website at http://jumpstartmarketing-concepts.com. We offer tons of training at no cost that will help you along the way in your online marketing journey. You can also link up with us on email at info@jsmarketingconcepts.com or any of our social media websites to include Facebook, Twitter, Pinterest, LinkedIn, YouTube, and Google +.

If you are interested in working with me direct for advice and mentorship you can set up a free strategy session any time at http://workwithjasonmiller.com.

Thank you for taking the time out of your busy schedule to educate yourself. Education is important to your business success! Now go Forth and Conquer!

## Our websites:

Main Corporate site: http://jumpstartmarketingconcepts.com
Patriot Team: http://patriotstobusiness.com

Patriot Community Outreach Program: http://patriotsoutreach.com

Secret Solo Ad Training: http://mysolosecret.com Work With Me Direct: http://workwithjasonmiller.com Join Our Patriot Team: http://patriotsignup.com

Patriot Community Outreach Program

Help someone that you know in need. This special card, when presented at most prescription counters, will save you up to 79% on the purchase of most prescription drugs. There is no obligation, no activation required and there are no fees to use this powerful card - just savings for the user!

In today's world of high prescription drug costs every little bit counts!

To learn more about this card, read testimonials of actual card users, download additional cards for your family and friends, and look up store locations and savings, visit our website at http://patriotsoutreach.com (This savings program is only available in the U.S.)

**HELP US HELP MILLIONS OF PEOPLE TODAY!**

**PRINT A CARD OR GIVE ONE TO SOMEONE WHO NEEDS ONE TODAY! HELP US SAVE MILLIONS OF $$ TODAY!!**

http://patriotsoutreach.com

www.ingramcontent.com/pod-product-compliance
Lightning Source LLC
Chambersburg PA
CBHW031358180326
41458CB00043B/6534/J